Resorts of the
Lancashire Coast

THE
LANCASHIRE
LIBRARY

KEITH PARRY

DAVID & CHARLES
Newton Abbot   London   North Pomfret (Vt)

British Library Cataloguing in Publication Data
Parry, Keith
The resorts of the Lancashire coast.
1. Seaside resorts—Lancashire (England)—History
I. Title
942.7´6   D670.L20
ISBN 0–7153–8304–3

Filmset in Monophoto Ehrhardt
by Latimer Trend & Company Ltd, Plymouth
and printed in Great Britain
by Redwood Burn Ltd, Trowbridge, Wilts
for David & Charles (Publishers) Limited
Brunel House   Newton Abbot   Devon

Published in the United States of America
by David & Charles Inc
North Pomfret   Vermont 05053   USA

Contents

Prologue 7
1 The Eighteenth Century 16
2 The South Port 22
3 Southport 31
4 Lytham 39
5 Fleetwood 51
6 Mid-Victorian Blackpool 60
7 St Annes-on-the-Sea 69
8 The Blackpool Trams I 79
9 The Blackpool Trams II 84
10 The Blackpool Trams III 92
11 Pleasures and Palaces I 99
12 Pleasures and Palaces II 112
13 The Blackpool & Fleetwood Tramroad 119
14 Blackpool's South Shore 132
15 Blackpool Promenade 137
16 Blackpool's Heyday 143
17 Blackpool Pleasure Beach I 149
18 Blackpool Pleasure Beach II 153
19 The Thirties 158
20 An Hotel's Story 163
21 Blackpool Illuminations 171
22 Morecambe 177
23 An Indian Summer for the Resorts 189
Epilogue 195
Index 199

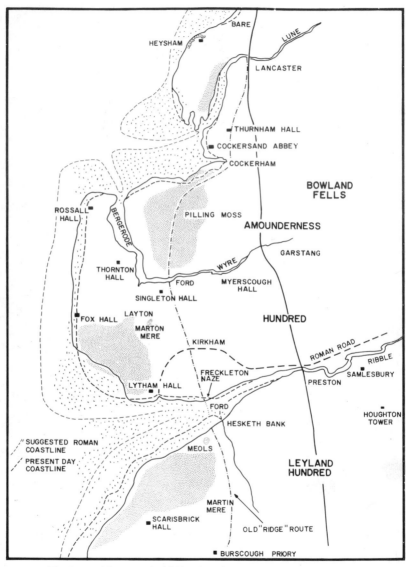

The Lancashire coast in 1610, taken from Speed's maps of the time

Prologue

On the face of it, the Lancashire coast is an unlikely place to find a chain of towns devoted to the art (or craft) of pleasure. It has no soaring cliffs or rocky coves, no fishing village harbours or brooding castles high on a headland. Its one bay—Morecambe—is huge, not intimately crescent-like in the fashion of Llandudno, Torquay or Douglas. Its one harbour—Heysham—is strictly utilitarian, and its haven—Fleetwood—equally so. In the main its old village 'hearts' were long since submerged by a tide of town development. Meols and Churchtown gave way to Southport, Poulton-le-Sands gave way to Morecambe, St Annes-on-the-Sea gave a new name to Cross Slack and Blackpool swallowed up Marton, Layton, Staining, Bispham, Warbreck, Norbreck and Anchorsholme.

The sea dominates, still shaping the coast, receding at Southport, hurling itself at the cliffs to the north of Blackpool, advancing and retreating through the centuries. The river-estuaries divide the coast, the Mersey to the south, and the Ribble, Wyre and Lune, parcelling the land in between, giving each portion its own identity.

And each resort—Southport, Lytham St Annes, Blackpool, Cleveleys, Fleetwood and Morecambe—has its own special atmosphere, its own appeal. It was an unpromising, uncompromising coast, yet it produced a string of towns whose main aim was to please, to give delight and relaxation. That is their common heritage.

We tend to think of the resorts as Victorian, just as 'industrial' in their way as Bolton or Barnsley (certainly the product of similar minds), but they have their roots in the eighteenth rather than the nineteenth century and the roots go deep into an older soil. This is Lancashire, historically remote, alien and perverse, the heartland of the Old Faith, the Red Rose County of John of Gaunt where the loyal toast is still to 'the Queen, the Duke of Lancaster'.

'The North', and therefore Lancashíre, had always been a separate place. For the Romans it was less a colony, more a military area, with Ribchester producing pottery, Mancunium on the Irwell an industrial centre, forts along the roads across the hills and north to the wall at the extremity of their empire. From Ribchester a road ran west across the Fylde towards the legendary Portus Setantii.

Legends of early Christianity drift up and down the coast like sea-mist. St Patrick himself, it is said, was shipwrecked at Heysham Head and the ruins there are of a chapel built by him. Similar legends tell of a chapel built at Kilgrimol (between Blackpool and Lytham) and washed away by the sea. Fact tells of the church at Poulton-le-Fylde dedicated to St Chad, a Northumbrian saint in the Celtic tradition, a pupil of Aidan at Lindisfarne and Prior in 664 AD.

The Anglo-Saxon Northcountry was infused with Danish and then Viking settlement. Danes settled an area of south-west Lancashire and Vikings came from Ireland via the Isle of Man to the coast—not as invaders, but as settlers. Their place-names are scattered all across Lancashire—Skelmersdale in the south-west, Rochdale in the south-east, Lonsdale in the north, Norbreck, Warbreck, Scarisbrick—and Sunderland. There are two other 'Sunderlands', one on the north-eastern coast of England, one in southern Norway.

Briefly, and gloriously, the North was a separate country—the Danelaw—with its capital at Jorvik, the present-day York. 'England' ended at the Mersey (and some would say it still does!). There are Viking tombs at Bolton-le-Sands, just north of Morecambe, and the splendid hogs-back tomb in Heysham church. Scandinavian crosses mark the trackways of those years—heading east to Jorvik, rather than south into England.

In an attempt to subdue and contain the Danelaw, Harold of England marched north and fought a battle with Harald Hadrada at Stamford Bridge. William of Normandy invaded, and Harold's army, exhausted by the forced march from Yorkshire to Kent, lost the Battle of Hastings. Had the punitive expedition not taken place England might never have been Norman.

Lancashire became nominally—but only nominally—the property of the Norman Roger de Poitou. The North was turbulent and it is said that Duke William himself marched north to subdue the northern counties 'swearing by the Splendour of God that none of his enemies would survive'. The Domesday Book, compiled twenty years after the invasion, records that of sixty-one villages in Amounderness 'sixteen are inhabited by a few people, but it is not known how many people there are. The rest are waste.'

Gradually, very gradually, Lancashire recovered from the devastation, but it was never completely Norman. The Viking language survived and there are barely a handful of truly Norman place-names in the whole county. It was a place of forest and marsh, a few small towns and a scattering of villages, held together by a primitive framework of feudal overlords and widely scattered churches owing their allegiance to the abbeys and their priories.

The remoteness of Lancashire and the sparseness of its population may have been the reason for the comparative failure of the Reformation to take hold there—certainly it was a contributory factor. Most of the gentry remained staunchly true to the Catholic faith; nearly all the manor houses had their own chapels and resident priests, and the laws relating to (Protestant) church attendance were particularly badly kept in Lancashire. The recalcitrance was tolerated until, in 1569, many Lancashire Catholics were involved in 'the Rising of the North', the rebellion designed to replace the Protestant Elizabeth with the Catholic, Mary, Queen of Scots.

The rebellion failed to attract support outside the North and the reprisals were immediate—something over 800 people were executed for their part in the rising, although one of its instigators, Sir John Southworth of Salmesbury, near Preston, was allowed to return to Lancashire even though he refused to convert to Anglicanism.

But from this time on, the Catholics of Lancashire became suspect, not merely members of an alien faith, but positive subversives. One of the earliest maps drawn of the county was designed to show where the suspect Catholics were. Punitive measures were increased but the Lancashire gentry still clung to their Catholic faith. Rossall Hall, then on the remote Fylde Coast, became the nerve-centre of English Catholicism, the Fylde itself its heartland. William Allen, the recusant priest whose family home it was, found it expedient to leave the country. In 1568 he founded the college at Douai from which Jesuit priests were smuggled back to England, often to Rossall. Halls and manor houses across the county had their 'priest holes', always ready to receive a priest passing from 'safe house' to 'safe house'.

The Lancashire Catholics' allegiance was transferred from Mary Queen of Scots to Philip of Spain and many would have supported his invasion actively. Philip of Spain saw William Allen as one of Elizabeth's most dangerous enemies and it was he who suggested Allen should be made a Cardinal. He wrote of him:

> He has morals, learning, judgement, great acquaintance with every-thing in the Kingdom and with the negotiations for its conversion and the instruments of all these have been and are his disciples, of whom so many have suffered martyrdom. The purple of his hat may be said to be dyed with the blood of martyrs whom he has educated.

Not without reason was Lancashire known as 'Catholic Lancashire' and it was referred to as such by Pope John Paul on his visit to the county of 1982. Nonconformism, the power which moulded the Industrial Society, was yet to come; 'historic' Lancashire meant the west, from the hills to the old road to the north and on to the wild coast on which the resorts now stand.

The Daltons were established at Thurnham Hall near Cockerham, the Allens at Rossall, the Cliftons at Lytham, the Southworths at Salmesbury; they and a score of other families clung tenaciously to their Catholicism with a fervour which bordered on obsession. During the Civil War they formed an uneasy alliance with the Royalists—Protestant, but seen by the Catholics as a preferable alternative to the Puritan Parliamentarians. Thomas Tyldesley of Myerscough was killed at the Battle of Wigan Lane in 1651 and his son, Edward, built a house between Rossall and Lytham—the marshes on the landward side, the sea behind—where he would be safe from government spies. This house, Fox Hall, could be said to be the beginning of Blackpool; it still exists, entombed within the walls of the present-day Foxhall

Hotel in the very centre of Blackpool's glittering promenade.

The recalcitrance and subversion—and the persecution—continued. The revolution of 1688 which deposed James Stuart and brought William and Mary to the throne found little favour in Catholic Lancashire, and when James landed in Ireland as a first step to recovering his throne, there were active steps in Lancashire to support his expected invasion of the mainland. Once again, emissaries landed secretly on the Lancashire coast at Cockerham to prepare the way—and once again the rebellion failed. James was defeated at the Battle of the Boyne, the conspirators in Lancashire were apprehended and put on trial in Manchester. Surprisingly, all were acquitted. Louis XIV, who had supported James, made peace with William of Orange and the voices of dissent were stilled, but only for a while.

The exiled Stuarts found sympathisers in Lancashire as well as in Scotland. Secret meetings with toasts to 'the King over the Water' (the participants passing their glasses over the finger-bowls in symbolic reference) were common, and plans were made to restore the Stuart line. Edward Tyldesley, grandson of Thomas, had a secret room prepared in Fox Hall to receive the King when he arrived. His role as a principal Jacobite agent was later taken over by John Dalton of Thurnham. It was a time of confused and divided loyalties. Even John Byrom of Manchester, staunch upholder of the Congregational faith (author of the hymn 'Christians, Awake'), was moved to write:

> God Bless the King, I mean our Faith's Defender,
> God bless, no harm in blessing, the Pretender,
> But who Pretender is, and who is King,
> God Bless us all, that's quite another thing.

So when James III swept down from the North, Lancashire welcomed him. He was feted in Lancaster and on 8 November 1715 a service of celebration was held in St Mary's priory church. Even though the invading army had only crossed the Lune the day before George I's name had been erased from the prayer book and James III put in its place. Balls were held and many ladies lost their hearts to the handsome Jacobite officers.

It was the same at Preston. A diarist of the time recorded 'The ladys in this town are so very beautiful, and so richly attired that the gentlemen soldiers from Wednesday to Saturday minded nothing but courting and feasting.' But those four days were crucial; they gave the government forces time to organise and by Saturday 12 November two armies were converging on Preston. The Jacobites lost the battle of Preston, over 1,500 prisoners were taken, order was restored and the trials began.

Thirty-six Lancashire rebels were sentenced to death and the executions took place in widely separated parts of the county so that the populace could see what happened to those who challenged George I. Twelve were hanged at Preston, seven at Wigan, five at Manchester, four at Liverpool, four at Garstang, and the rest at Lancaster, where their severed heads were impaled on the castle gateway. Many of the leaders, the Catholic gentry, were executed, others given long prison sentences. It is said that after his release, John Dalton, at one time one of the most powerful and well-respected landowners in Lancashire, walked the 250 miles back to Thurnham Hall. In the grounds he saw an old woman, gathering sticks for her fire. He failed to recognise her as his wife and she too failed to recognise him; privation had so scarred them both.

Thirty years later, the Jacobites were back, headed now by Charles Edward Stuart. The welcome this time was more cautious, if no less sincere. The army stayed the night in Lancaster, then moved off down the old road to Preston, meaning to go on south to the Mersey, crossing at Warrington. But the bridge there had been demolished, so they swung east towards Manchester. Invader though he was, there was a fascination about Charles Edward Stuart and his arrival in Manchester was not altogether unwelcome. 'Beppie' Byrom, John Byrom's daughter, recorded in her diary on 30 November 1745:

> I dressed me up in my white gown and went up to my Aunt Brearcliffe's and an officer called on us to go and see the Prince; we went to Mr Fletcher's and I saw him get on horseback and as soon as he got on he [the horse] began a-dancing and capering round as he was proud of his burden, and when he rid out of the court he was received with as much joy and shouting almost as if he had been King without any dispute, indeed I think scarce anybody that saw him could dispute it.

The Jacobites moved on south as far as Derby; nothing, it seemed, could stop the incursion. In London, shops closed, citizens rushed the banks, withdrawing their money, prepared for invasion and the restoration of the Stuarts.

But by 9 December, the Jacobites were back in Manchester, defeated and dejected. Charles Edward Stuart, it is said, refused to lead the retreating army but rode at the rear, sad and rejected. At Carlisle, 200 men recruited by the Jacobites in Lancashire made a last desperate effort to fight a rearguard action. They held the city long enough for Charles Edward Stuart to get over the border into his beloved Scotland. But that was all, and trials and executions followed once again. Charles Coppock, who had become chaplain to the Prince in Manchester and had been appointed Bishop of Carlisle by him, was hanged, drawn and quartered. Two other Manchester men were sentenced to be 'severally hanged by the neck, not till they were dead, but cut down alive, then, their bowels to be taken out and burnt before their faces and their bodies severally divided into four quarters'. Their heads were displayed in Manchester as a further warning to the populace.

Yet the Industrial Revolution was already making its presence felt in the Pennine valleys and across the plain of south-east Lancashire. Within a very few years the trials, tribulations, persecutions and terrible deaths would seem as remote as the longships of the Vikings.

The benefits of sea-bathing had been extolled for many years before; in 1702 Sir John Floyer, together with Edward Baynard, published a *History of Cold Bathing*. Sea-bathing could, it was said, cure cancer, rheumatism, ulcers, deafness, asthma, hernia, corns, leprosy, consumption, venereal diseases, tumours, a disordered mind and sundry other ailments. It also had one further advantage:

> Cold bathing has this good alone;
> It makes Old John to hug Old Joan!
> And does fresh kindnesses entail
> On a wife tasteless, old and stale.

A certain Doctor Russell published his *Dissertation on the use of Sea Water* in 1752 and insisted that the sea was a universal remedy, particularly if used in conjunction with one of his own preparations incorporating such delicacies as crabs' eyes, viper flesh, snails and tincture of woodlice. He further suggested that a pint of sea water drunk each morning would produce 'three or four smart stools' and insisted that immersion in the sea would complete the treatment. But he warned:

> A perfect repose for the body, and calmness of the mind is to be observed before the use of the cold bath, and all exercise of the parts affected must be forborn, that the fibres, by these means, when they contract themselves, may have the greater force to overcome any obstruction.

The older inland spas began to give way to the coastal bathing places. The south coast was the natural place for the London bathers to 'resort' to; Brightelmstone was ennobled by the Prince of Wales and by the early 1780s sea-bathing was all the rage. The fashion spread and the bathing places multiplied. By 1786 Yates' map marks a hotel, Mr Forshaw's, and a 'Bathing Place' on the Fylde Coast at 'Blackpool'.

To find such bathing places on the coast of Lancashire, still remote and mysterious, is odd enough, but to find one worthy of mention on a map such as Yates' *in the Fylde* virtually defies explanation. It was an alien, suspicious place, utterly remote and literally 'the back of beyond'. Some drainage had taken place but it was still a land of moss and marsh, windmills holding the wind that blew eternally across the wide acres under a huge sky. What roads there were corkscrewed between the fields and round the mosses, and the local people, isolated by their remoteness and their history of subversion and repression, could hardly be called welcoming.

Physically, it was separated from the 'mainland' by the estuaries of the Ribble and Lune and was itself divided by the Wyre. Psychologically, the Fylde was eons away from the merriment of Brightelmstone or the elegance of Bath. The Fylde, for all its religious heritage, was riddled with superstition, boggart haunted and clinging to old customs that were substantially pagan. The village wisewoman cured ills, cast spells, removed warts, told fortunes and dispensed medicines with equal ease; the old feasts were kept, loaves were marked with a cross, 'hag' stones were hung on stable doors to ward off evil—and all this within a handful of miles of the family home of the indomitable Cardinal Allen.

And it was here, of all places, that the architects of pleasure developed a town that led, and still leads, that plays host to the party conference as well as the millions of fun-seekers. The peculiar mixture of history, landscape and people known as 'heritage' gave a *lack* of history in its concrete sense, a landscape that had the quality they needed—space—and people who were inventive, resourceful and, above all, free. The same sort of people existed elsewhere in the North. In East Lancashire and Yorkshire they built the mills, the railways, the mines and the Industrial Society. On the coast, and particularly on the Fylde Coast, they built the pleasure palaces, hotels and boarding houses the Industrial Society needed for its brief hours of relaxation.

To the east of the old road to the North lay the hills and the developing industrial towns; to the west lay the sandhills and marshes. Midway between the Mersey and Morecambe Bay, topped and tailed by Lancaster and Preston, hemmed in by the hills and edged by the sea lay the Fylde—totally separate and tantalisingly exposed. Its geography had isolated it from the mainstream of development, its history had separated it completely. As Lancashire was (and, for that matter is) more a country than a county, so the Fylde was a province, rather than 'the field' its name implies.

1 The Eighteenth Century

A commodious, genteel house, but on a level, dreary, moorish coast, and 3s a day exclusive of liquors

The coastal towns are quite separate from the neighbouring wild Fylde countryside, which itself was historically separate from the rest of Lancashire. Linked by a slim life-support system—17 miles of road, rail and motorway from Preston—the towns are intensely, almost ostentatiously, *urban*. Fleetwood, for all its bow-wave of seaside pleasures and dockside activity carries itself like an inland town, Cleveleys like some city suburb, Lytham St Annes like a spa town or small university city. Gardens are planted luxuriously and are curiously formal with not a hair out of place, with not a hint of the Fylde hovering at the end of the road or across the railway.

Blackpool dominates physically, if not philosophically, like some huge luxury liner nosing its way into port, flanked by private yachts and a trawler or two. As one enters the town, the sophistication is sudden and intense—Porsches in driveways, miniature poodles yapping at gyrating lawn-sprinklers, antique shops thrusting their wares on to broad, tree-shaded pavements. The split-level ranch-style houses of the seventies push hard against the semis of the thirties which in turn run up against the bow-windowed, leaded lighted extravagancies of the early 1900s. There is spaciousness, yet no room to spare. The crowded town sweeps up, then down to the Promenade and the ultimate contrast between the land and the sea.

The Fylde is hidden, the past only occasionally glimpsed. Yet Blackpool has a past, submerged, as it seems to be, beneath the Victorian terra-cotta and Art Deco concrete. A shopping street has a vague, un-Blackpool-like kink in it, just before the broad bustling expanse of the Promenade, and this is it—Lane Ends, where the old road from Poulton met the Irish Sea.

In 1750, Bishop Pococke recorded after a visit: 'At Black Pool near the sea are accommodations for people who come to bathe';

there had been 'accommodations' since the early 1700s in the primitive cottages—about thirty of them—strung out along the edge of the beach, and by 1735 enough visitors were arriving to make it worthwhile for one Ethart a-Whiteside to set aside one specifically for them, but it was not until something like twenty years later that there were enough to encourage Mr Forshaw to establish the first hotel.

This stood on the site of the Clifton (on the corner of the Promenade and Talbot Square) and at Lane Ends there was another (which became the County and insisted for many years that *it* was Blackpoool's oldest). Lewis's Department store incorporates the site of this hotel. On the opposite corner was a cottage serving refreshments. This corner has seen many changes; the final one turning Montague Burton's into a restaurant—a reversion to the corner's original function.

Visitors were also accommodated further South at 'Old Margery's'—later Bonny's Hotel where 'genteel' accommodation was provided at 10d a day and at the Gynn Inn further north for 8d. By 1784 another hotel had appeared—'Bailey's' (on the site of the Metropole, now Butlin's) and the following year the proprietor was advertising:

Lawrence Bailey takes the liberty of acquainting the Public that he has completely furnished and fitted up a commodious genteel house in an eligible situation and that he hopes by his accommodation to merit the encouragement of such ladies and gentlemen as may be pleased to favour him with their company.

N.B. A bathing machine will be kept for the use of friends.

By 1787 the resort was firmly established, with other hotels advertising their attractions. Mr John Bonney was advertising that he had 'built a large dining room, with lodging room for 20 beds in addition to the House lately occupied by his Father-in-Law Mr Bickerstaffe, which has been fitted up in a neat and commodious manner for the reception of families during the bathing season.' Mr Sharples was informing the public through the *Manchester Mercury* that 'he had fitted up his house in a very genteel manner' and that he had eighteen lodging rooms and stabling for sixteen horses.

Prices had risen, too. Bonney accommodated 'Ladies and

Gentlemen' at 2s 2d per day each, children 1s 6d, servants 1s 6d—
'Table Beer' included. Mr Sharples was cheaper at 2s, children and
servants 1s 6d. Bailey's, acknowledged the best of the hotels (and
the most 'select') charged 3s 4d exclusive of liquors. Select it might
be, but 'Mr Forshaw's', not Bailey's appears on Yates's Map of
1786! Alongside is the legend 'Bathing Place' and 'Blackpool' (as
one word).

Bathing in the sea (and, for that matter, drinking it) was being
promoted as a health cure and this is what brought the visitors to
Blackpool; more than likely they needed some rejuvenation after
the journey itself! Canals might be licking out across the country
and the turnpike roads improving the old routes but once into the
Fylde the traveller was pitched into a maze of rutted tracks
wandering through the marshes, heading vaguely for a line of low
hills somewhere to the West. Expectations were not always fulfilled,
as Catherine Hutton found on her visit in 1788. It had taken the
Hutton family three days to get there from their home in
Birmingham and shortly after her arrival she wrote to a friend:

> You desire an account of Blackpool. You shall have it. Blackpool is
> situated on a level dreary moorish coast; the cliffs are of earth and not
> very high. It consists of a few houses ranged in line with the sea and four
> of these are for the reception of company. One accommodates 30, one
> 60, one 80 and one 100 persons. We were strangers to all, and on the
> recommendation of the Master of the Inn at Preston we drove to the
> house of 80 which is called Lane Ends. The company now consisted of
> about 70 and I never found myself in such a mob . . . These people are,
> in general, of a species known as Boltoners, that is rich, rough, honest
> manufacturers of the town of Bolton, whose coarseness of manners is
> proverbial even among their countrymen. The other houses are
> frequented by better company, that is Lancashire gentry, Liverpool
> merchants and Manchester manufacturers. I find here that I have no
> equals but the lawyers, for those who are my equals in fortune are
> distinguished by their vulgarity, and those that are my equals in
> manners are above me in situation. Fortunately for me, there is no
> shortage of lawyers in Lancashire, Preston alone containing 50; and
> there are always at Blackpool some whom I like, and with these I laugh
> at the rest.

The whole experience came as a decided culture-shock (as it so
often comes to strangers visiting the north for the first time).

Catherine was inclined to think, on reflection that:

> Boltoners are sincere, good humoured and noisy. The Manchesterians reserved and purse proud; the Liverpoolians free and open as the ocean on which they get their riches. I know little of the gentry but I believe them to be generous, hospitable and rather given to intemperence.

She found the wife of the Rector of Rochdale 'in person and manners resembling a good fat housekeeper . . . excellently skilled in pickling shrimps, potting herrings, raising goose pies and flourishing in pastry', but 'I daresay never heard of curry in her life!' Almost in spite of herself, though, Catherine had to admit: 'all ranks and both sexes are more robust than the people of the south. Hysterics and the long train of nervous disorders are unknown in the county.'

Catherine's ultimate mellowing may have had something to do with an encounter she had at Blackpool—not the first and by several million, not the last:

> I have had an offer here . . . The man is handsome, gentlemanly and agreeable enough, but he has been an officer in the army and a free liver, things totally out of my sober way. Your brother, who observed his attentions, says I am 'saucy'. I think I am not . . .

Catherine Hutton died in 1846 at the age of ninety—and unmarried (possibly regretting her hesitancy on that holiday in Blackpool so many years before!).

Catherine's father, William Hutton, had written Blackpool's first Guide Book *Description of Blackpool in Lancashire, frequented for Sea Bathing* (it had been published the same year that Catherine made her visit). Bearing in mind Catherine's romantic encounter her father's description of the parade on the promenade has a prophetic quality:

> Here is a full display of beauty and fashion. Here the eye faithful to its trust, conveys intelligence from the heart of one sex to that of the other; gentle tumults rise in the breast; intercourse opens in tender language; the softer passions are called into action; Hymen approaches, kindles his torch, and cements that union which continues for life. Here may be seen folly flushed with money, shoe strings and a phaeton and four. Keen envy sparkles in the eye at the display of a new bonnet. The heiress of eighteen trimmed in black and a hundred thousand pounds,

plentifully squanders her look of disdain, or the stale *Belle* who has outstood her market, offers her fading charms upon easy terms.

Father and daughter saw the same thing with slightly different eyes. Catherine refers to 'a few houses ranged in line with the sea and four of these are for the reception of company'. Her father is more specific:

> . . . about six make a figure, fronting the sea with an aspect exactly due west, and are appropriated for the reception of company; the others are the dwellings of the inhabitants, which chiefly form the background. In some of these lodged the inferior class, whose sole motive for visiting this airy region is health.

Catherine noted, and disapproved of, the table manners of her fellow holidaymakers:

> The people sat down to table behind their knives and forks to be ready for their dinner, while my mother, my father and myself, who did not choose to scramble, stood behind till someone more considerate than the rest made room for us.

The rigid meal time of the boarding house was, it seems, established in Blackpool the year before the storming of the Bastille! Her father suggests a solution—that every person seated at table before dinner should be fined one shilling. This money, plus that gained from fining 'any person vociferous after twelve' should be used for improving the sea front parade. William Hutton complained that 'disturbance reigns at midnight'; this time Catherine had the answer:

> My mother and I slept over the dining room and one night after we were in bed they [the other guests] were so obstreperous below that the noise was insupportable and ringing for the chambermaid I sent her with my compliments to the gentlemen, begging that they should not make quite so much noise as we were immediately over their heads. Not another sound was heard and I believe they went to bed to oblige me. Next morning before I could apologise for the liberty I had taken, they were all round me expressing their sorrow for having disturbed us and their ignorance that they were doing so.

Hurried meals, disturbed nights, a romantic, resisted encounter, (later generations of Lancashire visitors had a suitably evocative word for it—'clicking')—Catherine's holiday had all the ingredients of a future tradition. So had her father's note that the hotel charging 3s 4d did so 'exclusive of liquors' whereas the one charging 2s 6d charged extra for 'tea, coffee, sugar *and* liquors'—an early variant of the surcharge '1s for use of cruet' beloved of the later Blackpool landlady.

William Hutton's efforts to promote Blackpool through his guide went unrewarded:

> I was struck with the place, wrote its history, which was my fourth publication, price one shilling. The landlords met, agreed to take the whole edition, 720 copies, and I agreed to sell them at prime cost, sixpence each. Hudson [the then proprietor of the Lane End Hotel where the Hutton's stayed] and Bailey stood joint paymasters. These worthy gentlemen stationed at a distance [the Hutton's were in Birmingham] which often tries a man's honesty, obliged me to stay four years for the money. Bailey, in the interim, broke. Hudson would only pay his share of the nine pounds. The other I lost. We stayed here [Blackpool] near three months. My poor wife was attacked with an alarming fever.

2 The South Port

Handsome houses, green veils and lusty fellows under middle age

Across the Ribble estuary Southport (or, rather 'North Meols') too was wading in at the shallow end as a resort, but here the pattern was subtly different. A section of the Leeds & Liverpool canal opened in 1770 ran within 4 miles of the coast and gave easy access to it for the miners of Wigan and others from the hinterland. So the first visitors were not the middle class taking the ritualistic sea-water cures but miners and weavers on a jolly excursion by canal barge.

The visitors who needed accommodation found it at Church-town, but the best beach for bathing was at South Hawes, some two miles away along a shallow valley between the dunes. The bathers would go down in the morning and return in the evening; there were no facilities at the beach until, in 1792, William Sutton (who was to Southport what Forshaw and Ethart a-Whiteside were to Blackpool) built a crude driftwood shanty near the mouth of a stream at the 'Birkdale' end of the beach.

In 1797 Bold Fleetwood Hesketh ('Bold' is a family name, not a nickname) became High Sheriff of the County Palatine of Lancaster and the family moved from its home at Rossall to Meols Hall, considered to be more accessible and better suited to his high office. Visiting families found the area attractive and many bought plots of land and built houses, thus giving 'Southport' a residential as well as a resort atmosphere. Meanwhile, William Sutton had rebuilt his shanty and the new building had been almost jokingly named the 'South Port' hotel during a particularly energetic house-warming party.

The plots of land on which the visiting gentry built their houses fronted on to the lane leading from Churchtown to the beach and had been bought from the two lords of the manor; the lane was

22

therefore, christened Lord's Street—Lord Street after 1830. Then, when the shallow marshy valley was drained the lords of the manor insisted that the owners of the houses on the easterly side should extend their gardens across to the road and it was this area of private gardens the corporation later bought and which gave Lord Street its particular attraction.

For all that he owned the first hotel in South Port, William Sutton did not prosper and by 1803 he was languishing in Lancaster jail—committed there for debt. Two years later the word 'Southport' first occurs—in a lease granted to a Miss Bold on a site 'Adjoining in the East to enclosed land belonging to Wm Sutton called South Port'. The parish register uses the name from 1812 and maps of 1818 show it.

In 1825 the two lords of the manor, Peter Hesketh and Henry Bold-Houghton, were discussing various exchanges of land with a view to a joint development of the area. This degree of pre-planning and the resulting overall scheme gave Southport its particular character from the very start which was sharply at variance with the haphazard development of Blackpool. Just up the coast, at Fleetwood, Peter Hesketh took the opportunity to carry his town-planning aspirations further; the results were aesthetically satisfactory but financially ruinous.

By 1832 Southport had developed sufficiently—as much a residential as a holiday town—to publish its own history, printed and probably written by one William Alsop. He wrote:

Southport, at first glance, is calculated to fill the mind with admiration, especially the minds of those who delight in rural retreats from the noise and turmoil of a bustling town. It consists of one principal street nearly a mile in length, and upwards of ninety yards in width, composed of handsome houses on each side, adorned with gardens in front most tastefully laid out. When viewed from a distance it appears to be a long line of uniformly arranged buildings with scarcely one house projecting beyond another, but upon a nearer approach thereto, each cottage, or at least group of cottages, exhibits its own peculiar character, which presents an agreeable variety, which, from the extreme length of prospect, is lost, or unobserved in the distance. With respect to the buildings the visitor must be devoid of sensitive feelings that cannot admire the variety here presented to his view. Not only will the display of architecture attract attention, but also the gardens with a rich assortment of flowers, that occasionally shed forth their odiferous scents.

Southport must, indeed, have been a haven of peace, far removed from the stinking smoke-shrouded industrial towns wrecked with riots, haunted by the spectre of the Chartists marching, threatened by the belching locomotives of the new railways.

The History informs us that:

The salubrity of Southport arises in some degree from the absence of any substratum of marl or clay, but being sand to an indefinite extent, it receives the rain almost as speedily as it descends from the heavens; hence, parties may walk out clean and dry immediately after the heaviest shower.

A 'sandy sub-soil' was being extolled by estate agents a good century later. However, there were disadvantages to the sand:

Being of such an extremely fine sort, it becomes easily drifted by the wind, and consequently a source of some little annoyance to those who may never have been accustomed to anything of the kind; but, as with other matters, custom soon becomes akin to nature, and the inconvenience is not so much experienced after a few weeks' residence in this land of sand. The ladies, however, do well to wear veils here the year around, not so much as to hide their external charms, as a preservative for the eyes; green ones, in the heat of summer, would be recommended in preference to others, owing to the powerful reflection of the sun upon the sand.

The sand must, indeed, have been a power to be reckoned with in the early Southport. The town had developed along the shallow valley parallel to the sea and the sandhills, only a few yards away, extended the full length of Lord's Street. To reach the beach one had to cross them—and, after all, for all its flowers and quiet charm Southport was a bathing resort as well, but once there:

the shore at Southport is, undoubtedly, the best in the kingdom; being of gradual descent for more than a mile before we reach low water, and is free of shoals or quicksands. Bathing machines, in goodly order and number, are here employed. They are upon a new construction, being mounted on four wheels. On this plan, the danger of turning the machine in the water is thus removed—being made to return to the shore without turning. The owners of the machines are remarkably attentive and obliging, each striving to excel in arrangements for those who are desirous of bathing.

Decorum was to be observed at all times on the bathing beaches; gone were the raunchier earlier days when bathing was permitted in the nude and there was little or no segregation of the sexes. At Blackpool a bell was rung to warn gentlemen to retire from the beach as the ladies approached for their immersion; a second bell summoned the men for their dip—by which time the ladies had removed themselves to a safe distance. Any man attempting to take an illicit peep risked a fine—a bottle of wine for the company of the hotel; ladies were not so penalised (which gives a peculiar twist to the idea of equal opportunities!).

At Southport in 1832 things were not only governed by regulation, they were *seen* to be governed—by rules and regulations painted on a board:

1st. There shall be a vacant space of one hundred yards between the bathing ground appointed for ladies and that appointed for gentlemen; which ground shall be marked out by posts, with proper inscriptions on them.

2nd. Any owner of a machine going out of the line opposite the front and back posts, to be fined five shillings each time he goes beyond the bounds.

3rd. Any pleasure boat, or other boat, coming within thirty yards of any machine, out of which any person or persons are bathing, the owner of the boat to be fined five shillings for each offence.

The fines were substantial—something like a week's wage (and higher than a possible bribe to break the regulations!). A fourth regulation covers the possibility of something unpleasant happening to a bather—one gets the feeling it must have happened to someone immediately before the regulations were drawn up:

4th If any fisherman throws out of his boat any entrails of fish, or any dead fish, or leaves them on the shore without burying them in the sand to be fined five shillings for every offence.

A fifth regulation has a curious ring to it (again, as if the regulators were writing from bitter experience) and tails off as if the authorities are not quite sure of the penalties:

And any person or persons undressing on the beach, or on the hills, or crossing the shore naked, within one hundred yards from the two outside posts, will be dealt with as the law directs for the punishment of such offences.

Clearly, the most stringent efforts were being made to preserve decorum, which is curiously at variance with an account written three years after the regulations were featured in Alsop's book when there is a reference to:

squealing, giggling, kicking, splashing and wincing young ladies . . . [being 'dipped' by the bathing machine owners who were] stout, lusty fellows under middle age.

A Miss Weeton observed that bathing had been 'sadly exposing . . . gentlemen and ladies' machines standing promiscuously in the water . . . The bustle, hurry and confusion are most extremely disagreeable; the only comfort is that amongst such a crowd one may pass un-noticed perhaps.'

The bustle and confusion reached its height on the first Sunday after each 20 August—'Big Bathing Sunday' when upwards of 40,000 visitors would arrive—notably contingents from the Wigan coalfield (no doubt also 'lusty fellows under middle age') for the sole purpose of bathing. A piece of doggerel from the time declares:

. . . at noon behold a band
Of lovely maidens troop along the sands,
With eager haste approach the water side,
To give a welcome to the flowing tide—
Y'clad in flannel dress of blue and red
An oil case-cap as covering for the head:
When, like the Naiads, as we read at school,
They quick descend and trouble well the pool;
Heedless of being seen by vulgar men,
They dash and splash, and dash and splash again . . .

The sea itself solved the problem of decorum on the beach by gradually retreating from the town. In 1835 Peter Hesketh Fleetwood, the local landowner, was involved in the formation of a company intent on 'building a sea wall and founding a handsome marine promenade and building site fronting the sea shore'. When the company was promoted the sea wall was a necessary defence and photographs taken twenty years later show the Promenade (for which a toll of 1d was levied) and a number of houses along it and the sea is still there—more or less. Even in 1860 when the pier was built its seaward end barely dipped in the water at low tide and had to be extended to a final length of 1,500 yards before it reached the Bog Hole—a deeper water channel—and steamers could call in at Southport.

The railway had arrived in 1850, first from Liverpool and five years later from Manchester, Southport was growing and consolidating both as a residential town and a holiday resort; in 1801 the population of the whole parish was less than 2,000, by 1861 it was touching 16,000 (Blackpool was barely a third of its size). It was a gracious, well-to-do, possibly smug community sensing itself envied by other towns, aware of its reputation as 'the Montpellier of England', aware that one of its hoteliers had, as he said, 'spared no expense in rendering this house fit for the accommodation of the wealthy and noble families'.

The American author Nathaniel Hawthorne (who was US Consul at Liverpool at the time) lived in Southport for ten months during 1856–7. His less-than-enthusiastic view of the town serves as a useful antidote to the fever of euphoric prose poured out by its local promoters:

> It is a large village, or rather more than a village, which seems to be almost entirely made up of lodging houses, and, at any rate, has been built up by the influx of summer visitors; a sandy soil, level, and laid out with well-paved streets, the principal of which are laid out with bazaars, markets, shops, hotels of various degrees, and show a vivacity of aspect. There are a great many donkey carriages—large vehicles drawn by a pair of donkeys; bath chairs with invalid ladies; refreshment rooms in great numbers—a place where everybody seems to be a transitory guest, nobody at home. The main street leads directly down to the seashore along which there is an elevated embankment, with a promenade on top, and seats and the toll of a penny . . . people riding on donkeys, children digging with little wooden spades and donkeys carriages far out on the sands—a pleasant and breezy drive . . .

So far, the description is accurate and fairly innocuous, and reads, in all honesty, like the description of a similar town in New England (and 'Southport' has a vaguely Connecticut or Rhode

27

Island ring to it); but any equating of Southport with Newport R.I. is dispelled. Hawthorne refers to the 'brown, weather-hardened donkey woman', he dismisses the sea-reed and sedge-banded dunes as 'coarse grass'. The town crier, he observes has a 'doleful tone'. He dislikes the organ grinder performing under his window and he refers to bagpipes 'squealing out a tangled skein of discord' and clearly does not approve of a 'Highland maid who dances a hornpipe'. He notes the Punch and Judy shows, the minstrels, the military bands—all the colourful trappings of the traditional English sea-side resort and dismisses them all in one terse observation: 'In a word, we have specimens of all manner of vagrancy that infests England.'

By the 1880s, the sea had receded so far that enough stable land was available between the Promenade and the high water mark for there to be a proposal to build a railway along it, round the coast to connect with the Southport & Cheshire Lines Extension Railway then under construction. The concession to Southport was that the section alongside the promenade would be in a tunnel (presumably with ventilating shafts at intervals!). The proposal was opposed by the Corporation and withdrawn. Round about the same time came a proposal to build a railway from Hesketh Bank, just north east of the town, to cross the Ribble by a bridge and link with the railways to Blackpool. This time the opposition came from Preston (who were interested in improving the river for navigation). A later, tramway proposal was also made, which would have joined the Southport system to Lytham (and therefore Blackpool and Fleetwood), using a transporter bridge to cross the river near the old ford site at Freckleton.

On the land between the Promenade and the sea the Corporation built a splendid marine lake, later extended, which gives Southport one of its distinct attractions. The pier (which was, incidentally built by Brunlees, the man who had engineered the difficult railway line round the shore of Morecambe Bay) developed, with a splendid pavilion at its landward end offering 'High Class Varieties Daily' and excellent facilities for steamers nearly a mile away at the seaward end. Until 1897 when the record went to Southend, Southport's pier was the longest in the country; as with Southend, a tramway was built to transport visitors along it.

The sea continued to retreat. By 1923 the steamers could no longer tie up at the end of the pier and trips to Blackpool, North Wales, the Isle of Man and Barrow were a thing of the past. But as the sea retreated, the gardens advanced. Lord Street, now with mature and luxuriant gardens along one side had all the style (perhaps with half-closed eyes) of a Parisian Boulevard. Southport had attracted the best (and the most respectable) architectural design; Paxton, no less, designed Hesketh Park on an unpromising stretch of sand-dune offered to the town by the Reverend Charles Hesketh. A proposed bye-law prohibiting boys from climbing the trees was not proceeded with as it was assumed the trees would not grow high enough to climb. They were wrong—trees, flowers, shrubs, all grew ferociously in the unpromising sand. The town added botanic gardens in 1875, opened and closed other parks and gardens, and generally flourished.

A veritable civic centre—with all that that implied in expressed pride—grew up along a section of Lord Street; first, the town hall, a comfortably 'classical' building of 1852, then the splendid Cambridge Hall building opened by Princess Mary of Cambridge, Duchess of Teck in 1872—a suitably eminent personage and an eminently suitable style of French/German Renaissance architecture. Then, next door again, in 1878 came the Atkinson Library and Art Gallery, an uncomfortable marriage of both town hall and Cambridge Hall in style, but an impressive building nonetheless. Ten years later Science and Art Schools were built behind to complete the complex. The final addition to this proud group of buildings was a statue of Queen Victoria.

In retrospect, a Viennese, rather than Parisian comparison is more appropriate when considering the Southport of the immediate pre-1914 years. Photographs of Lord Street show ladies of Parisian elegance gently strolling under the trees—clearly none is of the *demi-monde*! The men in the photograph are elderly or in knickerbockered adolescence—any eligible man would have been whisked away by the Club Train of the morning, out of town along the straight, dead flat 10 miles of railway that led to the office in Manchester or down on the new electric railway to Liverpool. The glass canopies jutting from the shops emphasise the good things of life—food and clothes in Southport's case—Rowntrees' Café rubs shoulders with 'Mrs Molyneux' (a suitably grand name who must have displayed *manteaux et modes!*). Nearby are Thoms' Japanese Tea Rooms and Boothroyd's Store. If there is anything 'going on' in Southport it is behind the lace curtains, not out on the street, Parisian style! It is all much more 'apfel strudel' than 'champagne'.

Yet, something is there—an indefinable, un-English air of opulence and ease. Southport had its Winter Gardens (a huge Crystal Palace-like building advantageously set between Lord Street and the Promenade) linked to an equally impressive concert hall to give what they called 'the largest conservatory in England'. In Blackpool, Bill Holland had advertised 'Come and spit on Bill Holland's 50 guinea carpet' at his Winter Gardens; Southport people would not spit anyway and would expect the carpet to cost at least that! Where Blackpool was 'naughty' Southport was 'pleasurable'—and, on reflection, ever-so-slightly decadent. It is as if the whole town were built inside some vast conservatory.

And yet—the Balkans were erupting, the fleet of Dreadnoughts was in construction, Carson was arming Ulster, Emily Davison was flinging herself under the King's horse at Epsom, giving the Suffragettes their first martyr, there were coal strikes and dock strikes. Here, on Lord Street, everything is serene and sunny, and if the Emperor Franz Joseph were to stroll out of Rowntrees' Café no one would be surprised!

3 Southport

And stations to Whalley and beyond. Lytham and the Yagers.
Lord Derby and the Santa Ana

Although Southport never quite immersed itself in the swirling sea of holidaymaking, the mobility provided by the private car and the motor coach brought more and more visitors in the inter-war years. It was, like Morecambe, an alternative to the resorts of the Fylde Coast. A 'Captive Flying Machine' identical to the one erected at Blackpool's Pleasure Beach in 1906 appeared the same year in Southport, and it had a grander version of the 'Arial Flight' built at the Royal Palace Gardens in Blackpool. In the flight, visitors were drawn in gondola-shaped carriages suspended from a wire clear across the marine lake, but for all its popularity with visitors it was extremely unpopular with the residents of the promenade properties. It was erected in 1895 but dismantled, after protests, in 1911.

Southport had its funfair, though, with river caves, scenic railway, helter-skelter and a magnificent water chute, all in a pleasant setting by the lake. Gradually though, it was moved away to its own site and opened again as 'Pleasureland'. All-in-all, with its huge marine lakes, funfair, pier pavilion, sea bathing lake (as an alternative to the distant sea itself) and summer shows, Southport was a fully operational 'resort'. But its hugely successful flower show, open-air cafés and band concerts in the Lord Street gardens, its shops and, above all, its Lord Street gave it a combination of attractions which was unique and put it, almost literally, in a class by itself.

Liverpool reached out towards it, first by way of Waterloo (very nearly a resort in its own right in mid-Victorian days), Crosby, Ainsdale and Birkdale. The electric railway was fast and convenient. The first trains, advanced enough in their day with wide doors for quick loading and special luggage compartments with tambour-shuttered doors that could be opened before and closed after the train stopped at the station gave way to even smarter trains with power-operated doors for even speedier loading and unloading.

The line was built at incredible speed, too, the tender accepted on 21 March and the line from 'the sea-bathing village of Southport' to Waterloo—over 12 miles—opened on 24 July 1848. The link through to Liverpool came in October 1850. It was possible, even then to travel on to Manchester, but the building of the direct line in 1855 brought Southport within the orbit of that city also. It was this very accessibility which spurred the development of Southport as an upper-middle-class dormitory town.

Then another railway link came—from Southport to Preston. For the sandhills to the south of the town read the flat marshes of the Ribble estuary. But here there was no string of settlements capable of development to dormitory suburbs and the West Lancashire Railway remained something of an anachronism. Brunlees (of the Morcambe Bay line and Southport Pier) was engineer but here had few of the problems associated with the circuitous line round the bay or the shifting sand of Southport beach. Again, a Hesketh was involved, this time Sir Thomas George Fermor-Hesketh, Bart, one of the Southport residents promoting the line.

The railway promoters had prestigious plans. The line crossed the Rufford branch of the Leeds & Liverpool Canal (the Douglas Navigation) and in 1878 the railway company was authorised to 'build, purchase, hire, provide, charter, employ and maintain' steamers to carry goods, livestock and passengers from Hesketh Bank on the river Douglas to Preston, Lytham, Blackpool, Fleetwood, Barrow, the Isle of Man and along the Leeds & Liverpool Canal (which reached Wigan, Blackburn, and Burnley before crossing over into Yorkshire). It was this railway which also proposed a line along Southport's sea-front.

Railway plans at the time were grandiose and rivalries between the many independent companies intense. There was a plan to link the railway from Southport to the Manchester, Sheffield and Lincolnshire Railway's (later Great Central's) odd westerly extension from Manchester across Lancashire. There were plans to give a rival route from Manchester to Blackpool to cream off some of the Lancashire & Yorkshire's lucrative traffic, and proposals to extend the West Lancashire line (the magnificently named 'North West Central Railway') from Preston out to Whalley and Colne, over the Pennines to the Great Northern (another basically 'eastern' line) coming out from Bradford and Halifax to Keighley. None of these plans materialised, the West Lancashire was common to all plans and therefore continued to eke out a lonely existence ferrying passengers—and a very few passengers at that—across the lonely marshes along the Ribble estuary. By day the passengers would be able to see the buildings of Lytham St Annes glinting in the sun, by night the glow of Blackpool Illuminations—so near, so tantalisingly near, yet so far away.

The sandhills between Southport and Liverpool are a totally alien land, unique and with an utterly remote feeling about them, even though the commuter line is a mere mile or so away. They held city and town apart until 1974 when Southport was extracted from Lancashire and became part of the Borough of Sefton (a suitably prestigious name) and a strange coastal extrusion of the Metropolitan County of Merseyside; logical maybe, to the local government planners, but anathema to the residents of Southport.

It will be of little consolation to them to know that residents of Fleetwood find the linking up of their town to Garstang and the Bowland Fells as 'Wyre' equally illogical, that people in Lytham and St Annes do not feel themselves to be 'Fylde' and Wigan folk (for that matter all the inhabitants of the proud towns of South Lancashire) find 'Greater Manchester' a poor substitute for 'The County Palatine of Lancaster'. Wiganners at least have the consolation of knowing that the post office refuses to have Greater Manchester as a postal district so they are still in 'Lancashire', even though they're not!

Old allegiances die hard, not least among holidaymakers themselves. Morecambe will always be known as 'Yorkshire-on-Sea' even though most visitors will now come by motorway from the south rather than by way of the Midland Railway and the 'Little North Western' from Bradford and Leeds. Morecambe is preferred by some to Blackpool—or St Annes or Southport or anywhere!

They will point to the incomparable panorama of Lakeland mountains across the Bay, to the village of Heysham nearby, to the splendours of Lancaster a brief ride away. Morecambe would say that Blackpool is too big, too brash; Blackpool would say Morecambe was not big enough and needed livening up! Both could be envious of the other.

Lytham St Annes looks—enviously perhaps, at Southport across the estuary and nervously over its shoulder at its big, brassy (but *so* successful) sister round the corner. St Annes is Lancashire's newest resort—barely a hundred years old—a 'Company Town', the product of Victorian enterprise by way of the St Annes-on-the-Sea Land and Building Company Limited. Its neighbour, Lytham has a totally different 'feel'—medieval, manorial and still, though it is the beginning of the Fylde coastal strip, a feeling of the remote outpost of something. A booklet on sale in 1813 sums it up—it suggests the sandhills 'would offer most decided advantages to Yagers [Jagers] and Light Troops if their operations are intelligently and well led'. Marengo was just past, Waterloo, Elba and St Helena yet to come; Bonaparte was only a legend away across the wide open sea.

One senses the gentle shades of gentlewomen dreaming fearfully of 'Boney', of handsome ensigns dallying with the daughters of the gentry on the green lawns overlooking the estuary, of the constant watch on the horizon, the rumours of retreat from Moscow. Benjamin Britten could have made an opera of it!

Yet Lytham is older still. In the twelfth century it was the property of one Richard FitzRoger who assigned it to the church.

> For the salvation of my Lord, Earl John, and for the souls of my Father and Mother, and mine and my heirs . . . as a pure and perpetual offering to God and the Blessed Mary and St Cuthbert, and the monks of Durham, all my estate at Lethum, with the church of the vill., with all the things appertaining to it, in order to build a House of their own Order.

The Benedictine priory at Lytham would join its fellows—Burscough, Upholland, Cockersand Abbey, Cartmel and Conishead—strung out along the ancient trackway route from Chester and Stanlawe to Furness. That there was a monastic house here is a matter of history; when it was dissolved (in 1537) it was described as one of the 'lesser monasteries' and had an annual income of £43 3s 6d. But all traces of the priory have gone and even its site is a matter for conjecture. It may be on the site of the present Lytham Hall or it may be somewhere under the sea—a victim of the constantly shifting coastline.

At the Dissolution, Lytham Priory was granted to Sir Thomas Holcroft who sold it to Sir Cuthbert Clifton, and from then on the Clifton was welded firmly to that of Lytham. Clifton, like so many of the Lancashire gentry, was a Catholic—and remained so in spite of the persecutions of the Reformation—which makes the total eradication of the monastic buildings all the more 'puzzling'. Sir Thomas Clifton was one of a group of Lancashire Catholics accused of High Treason in 1594 and tried, and acquitted at Manchester after a period of incarceration in the Tower of London. A report states that in the year 1598 a nearby farmhouse contained some stained glass allegedly from the priory, but there is no report of the destruction *of* the priory in the previous sixty years. This tends to confirm the theory that Lytham Priory was destroyed by the sea, not by the zealots of the Reformation or by Clifton himself.

The Cliftons, although Catholics, or possibly because of the fact, allied themselves with the Protestant Derby 'For the King' at the time of the Civil War. 'Cromwell' meant Presbyterianism, Puritans—and repression. A Clifton died during the abortive Siege of Manchester under Derby's command, and his brother, Thomas Clifton was briefly host to Derby when the Royalist detachment under his command were involved in one of the most extraordinary exploits of that protracted and unhappy war.

A Spanish man o'war was reported run aground at the mouth of the Wyre, and in the nervous atmosphere of the time the wildest rumour could be taken for the truth. It was suggested she was an invading force, or reinforcements for the Royalists brought from Catholic Spain by the perfidious Lancashire Catholics.

The truth (or truth as far as it goes) is that she was the *Santa Ana*, a troopship destined for the Spanish Netherlands and driven off course by a gale. On 3 March a detatchment of 400 infantrymen left Preston for the Wyre intent on claiming the ship for the

Parliamentarians. The same day Derby arrived at the south side of the Ribble. The Parliamentarians held Preston but had left the old ford from Hesketh Bank to Freckleton Naze unguarded, and Derby used this route.

The *Santa Ana* meanwhile was trying to attract attention by firing her cannon. She continued firing for three days before any of the local people plucked up the courage to row out to the ship. Reassured that they were not being invaded, they guided the ship round the point and into the sheltered waters of the Wyre where the crew beached the ship and were then led across the sandhills to Rossall Hall.

Derby and his troop of cavalry stayed overnight at Lytham Hall and then headed for the Wyre, hoping to reach the *Santa Ana* before the Parliamentarians. As he crossed Layton Hawes (where Blackpool is now) Derby was observed by Parliamentarian scouts who, wisely, turned away, crossed the Wyre and headed north along the right bank.

Derby reached the *Santa Ana*, determined to destroy the cannon on the ship before the Parliamentarians got to her. He partially succeeded, setting fire to the ship which caused the gunpowder to explode. The cannon were either blown into the sea or fell into the hold. Then he moved across to Rossall Hall, collected some of the more important Spaniards and rode hell-for-leather for the Ribble ford. It was only useable at low tide and if he failed to cross he would be at the mercy of the approaching Parliamentarians.

The Parliamentarian force reached the Wyre to find the *Santa Ana* destroyed, but they managed to rescue the cannon—which they shipped up the coast to Lancaster. Derby returned to Lathom House, turned again, mustered something like 600 foot soldiers and 400 cavalry in South West Lancashire, rode back, crossed the Ribble and reached Lytham Hall. The following day he issued warrants ordering militia to assemble at Kirkham. With his own 1,000 men swelled to 4,000 by the Fylde militia he set off for Lancaster determined to recapture the cannon. By Saturday, 18 March, just two weeks after he had first slipped across the Ribble on his way to the *Santa Ana*, Derby lay seige to Lancaster.

So much is fact; the rest is conjecture. The *Santa Ana* was, it was said, blown off course. This she certainly was—a good 300 miles off course and half way up the Irish Sea. She had 'been blown' past the anchorages of Wales, past the Mersey, and the Ribble but had turned at Rossall Point. Had the captain mistaken the opening into Morecambe Bay for the Mersey or the Ribble? Had Derby been informed of the man o'war sailing north up 'his' coast and was this the reason why he rode in pursuit? Were these in fact reinforcements? Was it sheer coincidence that the men from the *Santa Ana* were taken to Rossall Hall, home of one of the most prominent Catholic families in Lancashire—and one closely connected with the international Catholic hierarchy? Derby collected the men from Rossall and took them south with his troops, but not as prisoners. Was it all *quite* as 'happenchance' as the records indicate?

Lord Derby failed to retrieve the cannon. The Parliamentarians had taken them into Lancaster Castle which was virtually impregnable. In any case Parliamentarian reinforcements were on their way from Preston. Derby could not take the castle, so he burned the city. He hid until the Parliamentarian troops were at Lancaster, then slipped round behind them and headed south for Preston.

He may not have been able to capture Lancaster Castle and take the *Santa Ana*'s cannon, but he captured Preston. Eighteen days after his first crossing downstream at Freckleton he was able to cross the Ribble openly at Preston. He wrote to tell Prince Rupert of his success. Or rather, he wrote in answer to a letter from the King's nephew, his wife's cousin.

> The Spanish ship which perished on the shore had divers goodly pieces of ordance in her, which by reason the enemy had them in possession, I thought good to spoil them if I could, and so did burn the ship; being advised by the Spaniards to do so, they knowing that their Master would well like that any ill might be unto the rebels of our King. I believe most now are useless, but a few may do us great hurt. You were mistaken, Sir, when you wrote to me in your last letter, that you conceived the Spaniards were with me, for I set them free . . .

Or did he? '*Their Master would well like any ill that might be unto the rebels of our King*'? Were the soldiers really meant as reinforcements for the garrisons in the Spanish Netherlands or had their master sent them as reinforcements for King Charles? Was the

Santa Ana driven by the gale past her landfall—the Ribble? In taking the desperate measures—the fast ride to the Wyre, the firing of the ship—was Derby 'destroying the evidence' as well as the cannon? Was a full shipload of Spanish soldiers simply set free to find their own way home?

The questions swirl in the mind like the mist over Lytham marsh; standing at Naze point—even today—it is easy to imagine that Spanish man o' war slipping silently in on the dawn tide bringing desperately needed help to Derby and Clifton, one Protestant, one irrevocably Catholic, both Royalists.

In 1968 a hoard of coins was discovered at Barton, just north of Preston. The hoard included two silver coins which had been minted for the Spanish Netherlands, together with one Spanish American silver dollar and a brand new English shilling. The facts remain—the wreck, the crossing and re-crossing of the ford, the seige of Lancaster, the capture of Preston. The hoard is fact, too, found on the route from Lancaster to Preston. The rest is conjecture. No one can prove the coins were hidden by (or perhaps stolen from) a Spaniard in the service of Derby, but no one can *disprove* it either!

4 Lytham

*The coach to the coast, for Hudson's, Bonny's and Hull's. Canals
for the commerce. Rails for the Fylde*

Although strictly speaking an estuary town, Lytham is set just
sufficiently 'forward' of the shore line to give the appearance of the
seaside. In 1799, one Captain Ratham observed 'Lytham is a
maritime village, which, since watering places have become so
fashionable a summer's lounge, is now advanced to a place of some
celebrity.' By 1813 the *Cursory Description of Lytham* was able to
record:

> The present village of Lytham, previous to its being frequented by
> bathers, was an obscure place, and from the houses being low and
> formed of mud and clay covered with straw, gave the stranger more the
> idea of an Indian town than the appearance of an English village. One
> circumstance above all must render Lytham dear to those who have a
> strict regard to morality—vice has not erected her standard here. The
> numerous tribes of gamblers, unhappy profligators, and fashionable
> swindlers find employment and rapine elsewhere. Innocent recreational
> delights, riding, walking, sailing and other modes of pastime banish
> cares from the mind, whilst the salubrity of the air expels disease from
> the body. Much diversion is found upon the two most excellent Bowling
> greens on which some part of the company are frequently seen enjoying
> themselves with a revolving bowl.

The holidaymaker had not yet arrived. The genteel middle-class
guests in the resort were like the 'company' at a country-house
weekend. The bigger Blackpool could still count its hotels on the
fingers of both hands and here there was some rivalry—the guests
from Forshaw's would studiously avoid the guests staying at the
inferior Hull's on the daily parade. But 'parade' they did, up and
down the infant promenade, in the manner of the spa towns.

A decade later, rented villas were available at Lytham. The old
Wheatsheaf Inn had been replaced by a newer, finer building and
the Clifton Arms charged 7s a day—1s less if the guest chose to eat

in the 'public rooms'. But Lytham was already looking back nostalgically to its golden days as an 'exclusive' resort.

> Bathers of the working classes came in shoals during the Spring tides from some of the populous districts of the county, when males and females were seen lining a considerable extent of the shore in promiscuous groups and not embarassing themselves about appearances.

The Industrial Revolution (and more importantly the Industrial Society) was developing fast. It had brought the need for better transport—canals, turnpike roads and the colliery railways made society mobile for the first time. In 1784 the *Manchester Mercury* carried the advert:

> Lower Swan Inn, Market Street Lane. The Manchester and Black Pool Coach. Sets out from the above Inn every Monday, Wednesday and Friday morning at six o'clock, dinner at Mr Cooper, the Black Bull Inn, Preston, where it meets a Diligence [a continental-style coach] which proceeds to Blackpool the same eve. Inside from Manchester to Black Pool 14s. Performed by Messrs Dixon, Cooper and Co.

The cost alone would eliminate all but the well-to-do; the turnpike roads had eased the journey somewhat, but it still took well over twelve hours to cover a bare 60 miles of fairly densely populated country. Not until the coming of the canals was it possible to move goods and people round the country reliably throughout most of the year—only a big freeze would immobilise the canal system.

The Bridgewater Canal from the mines at Worsley to Manchester resulted in a dramatic drop in the price of coal in the city and so stimulated expansion; the towns of Burnley, Blackburn and Wigan were linked to Liverpool by canal, then Wigan to the Bridgewater, the Bridgewater to the Mersey and to the Rochdale Canal, which was the first canal across the Pennines and one giving a more direct route from west to east—Liverpool to Hull—than the circuitous northern link by way of Burnley, Skipton and Leeds.

The coming of the canals affected Southport (the Leeds & Liverpool was a mere handful of miles away at Burscough and carts linked with the passenger boats there) but not the Fylde Coast. On the other hand Preston was a fast-growing town with thousands of

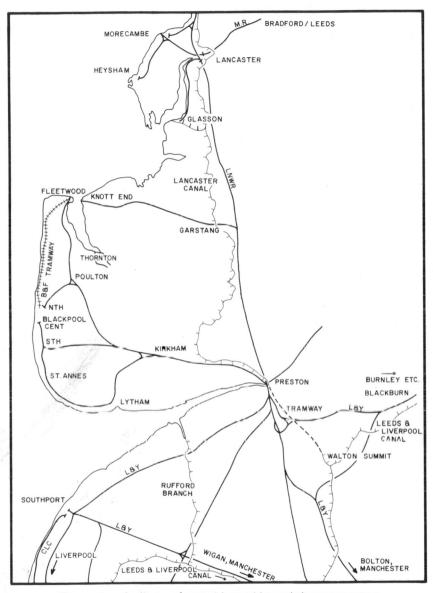

The canals and railways of central Lancashire at their greatest extent

the working classes sniffing the ozone on the westerly wind and eager to go down to the sea ten or so miles away along the improved roads.

The Lancaster Canal, important though it was, skirted the Fylde, following the 50ft contour and the Preston-Lancaster road. The merchants of Lancaster appreciated the value of a canal link when, in 1791 they petitioned the Mayor:

> The advantages the town of Liverpool has derived from their inland navigations, and so much increased from progress of the Canal towards Leeds, which is going forward with great spirit. The completion whereof and those projected cutts to Bury, Bolton etc., which are in agitation with little doubt of success, will add further benefit, and give merchants and traders in that place so decided a superiority in the vend of their imports as greatly to diminish the commerce of this town, and, in its consequences, materially affect the landed interests in the neighbourhood, unless some means can be found to meet them in the market upon more equal terms . . .

The northern half of the canal from Tewitfield to Preston was completed by 1797, then an extension northwards to Kendal. Next came a complicated series of arrangements by which goods could be brought north by way of the Bridgewater, Leeds & Liverpool and an isolated section of the Lancaster to Walton Summit, from which point a horse-drawn tramway led down to the Ribble and the basin of the northern section. Trans-shipment—barge to tramway wagon, then back to barge—inhibited the development of the canal; in addition, the canal remained unconnected to the sea—and the potentially lucrative coastal trade coming into the Lune and the Ribble. The high hopes, outlined in 1807 were never fully achieved:

> The canal on its track from Chorley to its southern termination passes through a country abounding with stores of coal, of which the parts on the northern end are destitute: on the contrary, the country north of Lancaster is full of limestone, of which the southern parts of Lancashire are in want. Cotton, sugar, rum and other West India produce are, by means of the canal, conveyed at an easy rate to the manufacturing and populous districts in the south part of the country.

Construction of the canal, and the all-important link to the sea, was delayed by the Napoleonic Wars. The main line of the Lancaster was not completed until 1819 and the branch to Glasson

Dock until 1826—the year after the opening of the Stockton & Darlington Railway. The *Lonsdale Magazine* commented:

> Owing to the very depressed state of trade [after the Napoleonic Wars] this canal has not been so advantageous to Lancaster as was expected, excepting in the article of coal, which is now brought up at easy expense to this and the neighbouring towns and villages.

The watering places, however, were prospering—though modestly. By 1824 there were three coaches a day from Lytham to Preston, a better road had been constructed over Freckleton marsh and in the season two steamers were bringing the 'working classes' down from Preston. Trade prospered too—albeit fitfully; the Ribble was still undredged and incoming ships had to tranship to lighters at Lytham or Freckleton. It was a fishing village also, although a visitor of the time was less than impressed by what he found:

> The sea here is supposed to abound with fish, but few are taken, and those principally with hook and line, the fishermen, either for want of spirit in not possessing proper boats to go out to sea, or not chusing [sic] to trust themselves on such a boisterous coast. The kinds generally taken here are chiefly salmon, cod, ray or skate, and flounders. The salmon is usually taken in the river, which is brought to the tables in finest perfection. Shrimps are taken on this coast in great abundance, and in supreme excellence. The river ells are obtained in plenty during the season which are remarkably fine. Many of the natives procure their livelihood collecting shell fish such as cockles and 'muscles' [sic] which they regularly take to Preston market every Saturday where they meet with an immediate and ready sale for their week's labour.

Blackpool, facing west and on an even more boisterous coast was developing slowly; in 1801 it took two days to reach the town from the eastern side of the Pennines! When the visitors arrived they found a tiny town, barely half the size of Lytham, with a resident population of under 500. In fact, 'Blackpool' contained less than that number—it was part of the parish of Layton-with-Warbreck—and the delights of its hotels could be set down (as they were in the 1790s) in one poem:

Of all the gay places of public resort
At Chatham, or Scarbro', at Bath or at Court,

43

There's none like sweet Blackpool, of which I can boast,
So charming the sands, so delightful the coast;

The houses are many, and all of them stor'd,
Not one but is able to spread a good board.
At Bonny's, at Hull's there's plenty of meat,
Their rooms and their beds are both cleanly and neat:
My friend, Mr Hudson stands next in the row,
From Buxton he came, I would have you to know.
The next house is Forshaw's, a building enlarg'd,
Good doings, no doubt, but you're sure to be charg'd.
The next house is Bailey's, so new and so neat,
Much pains he has taken to make it complete.
It stands on the beach far detach'd from the rest
And with a fine spring of good water is bless'd.
Old Ned and Old Nanny at Fumbler's Hill
Will board you and lodge you e'en just as you will.
The next house of fame that I now do take in
Is fam'd Billy Snape's 'Surs' they call it the Ginn;
He keeps a good table and plenty to eat
With whey in abundance to drink with your meat:
His servants are civil, good natur'd and mild,
You'll find none their like if you search the whole Fylde.
Then who's like friend Billy? 'Cum hither I pray,
And sarvants remember when you go away.'

Seemingly, a more boisterous approach than Lytham's. To some
extent, Blackpool limited its own development; existing landlords
bought up vacant land in order to prevent it being developed by
rivals, and in Lytham Squire Clifton achieved the same result by a
different method: until 1820 houses built in Lytham automatically
reverted to the Lord of the Manor after a mere forty years' lease.

By 1816, the first regular public stage-coaches were operating
between Preston and Blackpool and the journey from Manchester
was certainly more comfortable than it had been—though little
faster. The coach left the 'Star' in Deansgate at 8 in the morning,
was at Bolton by 10am, Blackburn at 12, Preston at 1.30pm, then,
after a respectable break in that town, Blackpool at 6.30pm. In
thirty years the journey time had been shortened by something like
three hours.

A visitor coming to Blackpool for the first time then found, as he
would find now, that other guests had been coming for thirty years.

It was still the custom, too, to virtually give a life-history to the other guests, but once accepted, he became part of what one called 'a sort of social society', exchanging 'every possible politeness and the civility of a brother or sister'.

The visitors still paraded on the grennsward above the beach, but this was now described as, 'now wasting away to a gravelly footpath'. Bailey's Hotel was now charging 7s a day, the Lane Ends (where the Hutton's had lodged in the 1780s) was much cheaper at 4s 4d, John Bonny's (further south but popular) housed forty guests and Butcher's hotel (on the opposite corner to the Lane Ends) was considered as respectable as most and more so than some! Blackpool was following the trend in letting off furnished houses and cottages and even Raikes Hall let off apartments. Being slightly inland, and therefore more sheltered, it was considered very suitable for those of a delicate disposition. The 'Yorkshire House' at the southern end of the promenade was considered decidedly inferior.

Blackpool was still barely a 'town'; it had no church of its own, although the first tentative moves had been made as early as 1789, and visitors and residents were obliged to go to Bispham for worship. A hotel set aside a room for Sunday services eventually, sometimes with a holidaymaking clergyman leading the congregation. There was a coffee-shop and a newsroom and at Bonny's Lane there was 'a noted potted shrimp shop, which may be purchased in dozens, in pots, to any order, and where you may purchase whey, a good cooling drink'. Nearby was the cottage where a Mrs Bundell made gingerbread—and a small fortune!

Smuggling was also a lucrative occupation for the Blackpool locals; contraband goods—the much prized brandy and rum for the parson and the squire of legendary England—came over from Ireland and the Isle of Man to be quietly off-loaded into rowing boats creeping out from the dark, deserted beach. The Fylde Coast natives were well-used to this kind of subterfuge; as the Catholic recusants had slipped across the dark marsh from 'safe' house to 'safe' house, so the kegs passed from hand to hand.

Vice may not have 'erected her standard' in Lytham, but it had in Blackpool (possibly that is why Lytham drew the comparison); the fortnightly fairs held at Lane Ends were excuses for wild drunkenness and debauchery—if the clerics of the time are to be belived. They railed appropriately at the excesses which 'met the eye and wounded the ear'. Variations on the theme of immodesty during bathing were included in many a thundering sermon, and suitable regulations were called for.

Blackpool's population rose very slowly, from 473 in 1801 to 749 by 1821, but the town was 'consolidating' all the time. The worst of the post-war depression was over, times were changing, tastes becoming more sophisticated and local residents were aware of the need to provide additional facilities for their summer influx. In 1827, the Lytham local paper observed:

> The following are much needed in Lytham—names to the streets, numbers to the houses, lamps for dark evenings, a public clock, a market, livery stables, gigs and horses to be hired by the hour, decent bathing machines, a news room and bath carriages to convey folks to church in wet weather.

Whittle's *Marina* published in 1830 remarks that there were at Blackpool 'at the flux of the season from eight hundred to a thousand visitors'. Nickson's hotel (the Clifton Arms) boasted an orchestra in the dining room and ballroom and 'four assemblies have been known to take place in one week during the bathing season extending from July to October'.

Lytham got its bathing machines, owned by two men who were, according to a contemporary observer, 'from long experience and constant practice . . . declared to be particularly adroit in delicately handling the fair females out of the machines into the water'. It is not recorded whether or not they were 'lusty fellows under middle age' as they were at Southport!

A fence now protected the visitor parading on the promenade at Blackpool and one or two of the hoteliers had placed seats outside their premises. The water-supply (albeit from springs underground) had been improved, there was a daily post in the season and new property erected on the sea front gave Blackpool, according to Whittle's *Marina*, 'when viewed from the sea a large and imposing appearance'.

Travelling theatre companies visited the coast now and one company was that of the Lardner family—father, mother, son and daughter. They offered such delights as Cibber's *Journey to London or a Bold Push for Fortune* and a 'laughable farce' *The Irish Tutor or New Lights.* Lardner *père* also offered 'likenesses in miniature at from two to five guineas' and the son gave lessons in 'the polite art of dancing'. Whittle saw one of their performances at Lytham and although the play itself was 'tolerably got up' he complained that the scenery 'was not of that kind which befitted a place of dramatic entertainment'. Clearly Mr Lardner's artistic talents were somewhat limited!

Whittle was admirably objective at a time when more local writers were breathless in their enthusiasm for the new resorts. He suggests that Lytham would benefit from a regatta 'on the principles of that annually displayed at Sunderland near Lancaster, it would tend to great and lasting benefit'. He joins the debate about public bathing suggesting that 'some rules be formed, as at Southport, to prevent men bathers shamefully exposing their persons to the great annoyance of females'.

He drew Southport into his comparisons again when he suggested that although Blackpool had 'a large and imposing appearance' its houses would benefit from the kind of verandahs, trellis work, climbing plants and so on, which he had noticed at Southport. Blackpool's reaction to this suggestion is not recorded, but can be guessed!

Whittle's *Marina* was published in 1830—and the same year, towards the end of the bathing season at Blackpool, the first trains began to run on the Liverpool & Manchester Railway, the first railway designed to accommodate passengers as well as freight. There was already a line between Manchester and Bolton, and within six weeks of the opening of the Liverpool & Manchester the survey was completed for a line across the Pennines from Manchester to Leeds.

All this was happening a long way away from the Lancashire Coast, but gradually, the railways crept nearer. By 1838 it was possible to travel from Liverpool and Manchester to Preston by way of Parkside junction on the Liverpool & Manchester, and Wigan; there were plans for a railway direct from Bolton to Preston. By 1840 the Lancaster & Preston Railway was open—railways running parallel to the historic route up from the Mersey, across the Ribble to the Lune.

Far more significantly, the Fylde had its own railway—part of the overall development plan proposed by Hesketh, at that time High Sheriff of the County Palatine. The Preston & Wyre Railway had been proposed in 1835 to link Preston to a creek at the mouth of the Wyre known as 'Cold Dubbs'. (Fleetwood was still very much in the architect Decimus Burton's mind's eye and on his drawing board.)

A single line opened on 15 July 1840 with a train leaving Preston at 11.50am, reaching Kirkham 25 minutes later and arriving at Fleetwood within the hour. It was all a far cry from the days when travellers invariably got lost once they headed west out of Kirkham! The narrow toll road constructed by Thomas Clifton and Sir Henry Hoghton, barely 12 feet wide, had given way to a superb new iron road, linking the Wyre—and therefore the towns over the sea from it—to Preston and beyond. Along this line, Preston & Wyre trains were running in both directions three times a day, and the directors of the railway proudly pointed out that connections were available to Birmingham and London. In the opposite direction a regular steamer service by *The Express* was instituted to link Bardsea, near Ulverston, with Fleetwood and the trains.

The canals and the major roads might have avoided the Fylde, but the railway did not. Admittedly, it ran from Preston to the Wyre, but that took it within 3 miles of Blackpool and 5 miles of Lytham. The consequences were to be felt almost immediately.

5 Fleetwood

Peter Hesketh and Decimus Burton. A grand design, but a most gloomy aspect

The Wyre estuary—the Bergerode—has been a safe haven since pre-Roman times and both Skipool and Wardleys were flourishing ports in the sixteenth century; there is evidence of trade with Russia and the Baltic ports in tallow and flax. By 1708 there were six customs officers assigned to the ports, working from a customs house in Poulton-le-Fylde, with three pilots stationed at Knott End to assist in the passage up the river. Timber was coming in from North America and iron from Furness. In the reverse direction salt from the pans at Salthouses was shipped across the bay to Cumbria. Salt manufacturing was carried on all round the coast (there are hamlets called 'Saltcotes' near Lytham in the south and Carnforth in the north). It was at the village near Carnforth that John Lucas observed the process in the eighteenth century:

> In hot weather during the neep tides they harrow with a Thorn or such like thing, the Flats that are always overflowed by the Spring Tides then scrim and scrape into Ridges which they take away in Caups and preserve under cover. Then put the Sand in Troughs lined with blue clay with holes in bottom and pour fresh water on which drains the salt with it into waiting vessel containers. So long as this liquid is strong enough to bear an egg they pour on more water and as soon as the egg begins to sink they empty the sand out and refill with fresh. The drained salt water is boiled on turf fires until only salt remains. They use leaden pans for boiling(!).

In 1825 it was recorded that the principal manufacturers of Kirkham (a linen weaving centre, hence the emphasis on flax) had 'large and commodious warehouses' at Wardleys on the eastern bank, and as late as 1876 Porter in his *History of the Fylde* was reporting that grain vessels had been unloaded at Skipool within the previous few years.

Until the coming of the railways the creeks at Skipool and Wardleys, well inland, were ideally placed for the distribution of goods throughout the Fylde. 'Fleetwood' (although there was no such place), at the mouth of the river was not; isolated and remote it seemed, although potentially it had first-class facilities.

The local landowner, Peter Hesketh, had succeeded to the Rossall Hall Estate there on the death of his father in 1824. In 1830 as High Sheriff of Lancashire (at the remarkably early age of twenty-nine) he was one of the spectators gathered for the opening of the Liverpool & Manchester Railway. A year later—to commemorate his descent from the family of that name—he assumed the surname 'Fleetwood' by royal warrant. From 1832 to 1847 he was first Conservative then Liberal Member of Parliament for Preston, and by 1835 he had been instrumental in forming a company to build a railway from Preston to the tip of the estuary close by his home. On this windswept rabbit warren of sandhills he proposed to build not just a harbour but a complete port and elegant watering place. Moreover, he employed Decimus Burton, one of the foremost architects of the day to design it for him.

Decimus Burton was responsible for some of London's finest structures; in collaboration with Nash, Soane and Repton (no mean combination) he had designed the street linking Carlton House with Regent's Park (one of the possible sites for a house for the Prince Regent)—the future Regent Street which was constructed during the years 1816–20. In 1828 he designed the 'colonnade' screening Hyde Park at its southern end and giving a grand ceremonial entrance to it; the following year he built the Athaneum, at the corner of Waterloo Place and Pall Mall. St Dunstan's Institute for the Blind, facing the Outer Circle at Regent's Park, a building for the Royal Humane Society in Hyde Park and the consumately skilful Palm House at Kew were to follow. What this sophisticated and experienced architect made of the barren waste at the mouth of the remote river in Lancashire is a matter for conjecture. Possibly he saw it as the ultimate challenge; undoubtedly he did some of his most 'mature' work here.

Burton incorporated the largest of the sandhills, re-named 'the Mount', in his plan and the streets of the town were to radiate from it. The streets were marked out—using a farm plough it is said—and the first stone laid at the corner of Preston Street and Dock Street (in May 1836 if the record in *Herepath's Railway Journal* for that month is to be taken as accurate; as the construction of the railway began the same month the reference may refer to the railway). The first completed building, it is said, was a public house on Church Street.

Hesketh Fleetwood was a realist; first the town needed working-class houses and pubs to fuel the dockside industry—the more genteel aspects of this 'Brighton of the North' could wait awhile. Decimus Burton may have advised on the matter of priorities; his father had been one of the architects of St-Leonard's-on-Sea, and that venture had failed because of the lack of commercial and industrial factors in the design.

Decimus Burton contributed to this early, mundane part of the scheme. The architect of the Athaneum and the Hyde Park colonnade turned his attention to the humble 'artisans' dwellings' to be erected in Upper Dock Street, Fleetwood (now Mount Street). At first sight they are architecturally undistinguished—simple terrace houses, a door opening straight on to the pavement, a window alongside, another above. They are devoid of ornament and obviously strictly utilitarian. They form two terraces facing—a street in fact.

The house at the centre of each terrace stands slightly 'proud' of the building line and each has a flattish gable in place of the normal eaves. A shallow 'string-course' runs along the front of each terrace—a suggestion of the more handsome decoration in grander terraces. The 'feel' is decidedly classical—light, graceful, pleasing.

In 1962, the houses in Mount Street were included in the local council's 'Limited Life Housing Programme' and by 1977 they were threatened with immediate demolition. As so often happens in these cases, it was only the threat of demolition which brought action from the conservationists. In October 1977 these houses, the only surviving examples of Decimus Burton's less prestigious work, were 'Listed' as being of special architectural or historic interest.

On 29 June 1978 the Council declared the street a clearance area, but the buildings stayed up pending a public enquiry, and at that enquiry the Inspector agreed that, on inspection, the houses were correctly represented as unfit houses but he was not satisfied that the Council had established a sufficient case to show that demolition was the most satisfactory solution. His report concluded:

> The special architectural interest of the buildings lies in the involvement in their design by Decimus Burton, the fact that they are among the earliest buildings of the town which still survive intact in the form indicated on Burton's layout plan, and their overall picture as composite facing terraces with central gabled features . . . the terraces still show features, lacking in other terraces in the locality which reflect in an austere way the classical principles of design, and in my view special efforts should be made to preserve them if reasonably possible.

The houses, ignored by the architectural pundits for so many years, were suddenly as firmly in the limelight as the most stately of Britain's many stately homes!

Burton's 'grander' structures in Fleetwood—more publicised and more easily appreciated by a *cognoscenti* steeped in the grand classical 'academic' tradition were never in danger. The 'appeal' of Queen's Terrace and the North Euston Hotel is immediate; the terrace facing the river has great style—the equal of anything in Bath or Brighton and in many ways superior to grander more expansive work. It achieves its effect by detail, scale and proportion—the real classical criteria—rather than by size and ostentation. Nearby is the curved facade of the North Euston (the name supplies an obvious and evocative link) Hotel. There are bigger and grander hotel buildings but few are so impressive; again it is a matter of scale and proportion. The word 'immaculate' springs to mind. Even the rear of the building (so often the worst part) has considerable architectural effect.

As Fleetwood was a port, Decimus Burton was required to design two 'tools of the trade'—lighthouses. In both cases he produced an architectural gem; the smaller, now used as a promenade shelter, is 'lively'—a jolly little pepperpot atop a neat colonnade with a balustrade round it. The other—the Pharos—is a more solemn structure altogether. Yet it has grace and again, great style. Burton did not simply design the lighthouse and plant it on the shore; he placed it symbolically in a (suitably) modest 'circus' at the intersection of Pharos Street and Lune Street (with, appropriately, Albert Street, Queen's Street and Bold [for Hesketh] Street nearby).

Fleetwood was, in fact too 'bold' for Hesketh Fleetwood. By 1841 he was forced to sell off his Blackpool estates, and in the following year those in Southport. The port and the watering-place 'worthy of the name' were not succeeding. In 1844 he left Rossall Hall and retired to the South of England. His lands in Bispham and Norbreck were disposed of and finally, when he died, his interests locally were taken over by the Fleetwood Estate Company, formed for the purpose. Decimus Burton returned to London to grapple with the problems of iron and glass construction for the Palm House at Kew.

The railway had arrived in 1840—at first along a 2 mile timber trestle bridge across the marshes between Burn Naze and Fleetwood. The two lighthouses were first lit in December 1840 and the first (iron) wharf opened in 1841. On 7 October of that year Sir Peter Hesketh Fleetwood was able to announce some good news: steamer services were operating to the Isle of Man, Whitehaven, Belfast and Ardrossan (for Glasgow). But the idealism of the early days was failing. The plan had been for Fleetwood to be a major port—that was not to be, it seemed. Locomotives were becoming increasingly powerful, able to tackle the steep gradients over Shap Fell to Scotland, so the sea link, carrying passengers round Cumbria from the north then speeding them to London by train would be redundant. The grand North Euston Hotel awaited its overnight visitors en-route from Caledonia to the capital—they never came.

A visitor to the town in 1842 found it presented 'a most gloomy aspect—a splendid modern ruin, no shipping, no steamers, no passengers for the trains'. Fleetwood had hotels, two churches, five or six streets of houses, a gasworks and a population of 3,000. It was also a port—officially (and Preston had been downgraded to the status of a 'creek'!). Yet it seemed the new town on the tip of the peninsula had no future. There was a brief flurry of excitement when Her Majesty herself put in and took the train from the new station (but even the usually punctual Victoria, blessed with fine weather wherever she went *failed* to arrive for several days. The crowds came, went, came again, went again and finally were able to see the diminutive figure crossing from the ship to the new-fangled train). Then the town subsided once again into its infant sleep. The North Euston—so often compared with Burton's masterpiece, the Athaneum, even suffered the indignity of being turned into a barracks.

Slowly, very slowly, the town grew. The fishermen, if not the gentry, arrived and trade revived. The visitor of 1842 observed in 1846 that there was now more work to do than the local labour force could handle and that railway receipts had increased from £100 to £1,500 a week. The coastal trade increased through the 1850s and this led to further grandiose plans being made. In 1869 a dock was begun—then suspended. Work began again in 1871 on a project that was to take six years and give Lancashire a new place name— Wyre Dock.

The railway line along the old timber trestle (which had caused passengers much alarm) had been replaced by a wide diversion inland, and it was on the land between old and new lines that the dock was built. It was 10 acres in area, 1,000ft long and 400ft wide. At the same time a 'timber pond' was built to store log-timber. The tide—literally and metaphorically—turned.

The railway—now the Lancashire & Yorkshire—was instrumental in developing the port facilities. A grain elevator was built, then a new station to handle passenger traffic (notably to the Isle of Man) with direct access from the platforms to the quayside. Fishing became more and more important. In these days before the home deep-freeze, 'fresh fish' was important and Fleetwood, with its excellent communications with the millions in the North West became a by-word for just *that*! 'Fleetwood' fish always seemed to reach the mill-town fishmongers just that bit fresher.

The town became a modest resort also. It developed the usual crop of hotels strung out along the sea-facing north side of the peninsula. A pier was built for the visitors (stubby, as if it did not wish to interfere with the channel sweeping round close inshore so that the steamers were a mere few yards from the Promenade) and the pier was free in the days when such things were usually not. The Blackpool & Fleetwood Tramroad arrived—a unique form of propulsion which gave the town an American air. The first terminus was in the middle of the road by the North Euston but subsequently (after Blackpool Corporation had taken over the line) was looped round to the ferry terminal and station. On the way back the line had to pass in the shadow of the Pharos; perversely, it passed on the *wrong* side of the road and many an unwary car-driver has been given an instant nightmare by the sight of a huge double-decker bearing down upon him!

Pleasant gardens developed along the Promenade, bowling greens, a marine hall with a summer show, a huge marine lake, hotels with a distinct touch of Blackpool's New South or Morecambe's East Promenade about them. But the town never quite went over to the holiday trade and never over-reached itself. In a sense, it kept the kind of 'scale' and 'proportion' in its development that Decimus Burton incorporated in his buildings. It has a Savoy Hotel—a neat, double-fronted Victorian house that would not look out of place in Harrogate.

Fleetwood is working class in the best sense of the word. It has had to work hard for its living—to survive indeed—and it shows the scars—again, in the best sense of the word. The fishing industry declined, revived, declined again. The dreaded Icelandic trawlers arrived and the Isle of Man boats left—the old wooden landing stage was simply crumbling away. Even the railway left. Fortified, no doubt, by its breathtakingly strong throat lozenges, exported world-wide and claimed to be a friend to all fishermen, the town fought on. Its market, of all things, became an attraction for visitors and the coaches flooded in from all over the North. The ferry across the swiftly flowing Wyre to Knott End was threatened—and survived.

Postal & Oriental (a name, surely, as grand as the North Euston) arrived—admittedly with a workaday container and roll-on-roll-off service across the Irish Sea, and the unthinkable happened—a new landing stage was built. The Isle of Man Steam Packet Company's ships (again a grand name) sailed back into Fleetwood. People wanting a holiday in a gentle, restful resort took Fleetwood to their hearts and the day-tripping car driver found the parking easy, the view (of ships and sea-and-cloudscapes) suitably-modestly stimulating. The splendid old North Euston, so long neglected, found new owners who appreciated it. There may be no 'Burton Street' in Fleetwood but there is something more fitting—a Burton Suite at the North Euston. Only the railway—the reason for the town being there in the first place—failed to return.

Besides being working class, Fleetwood is also eccentric—again in the best sense of the word. One cannot go *through* Fleetwood— only *to* it. In the shadow of its splendid buildings are cafés with the fare displayed—traditionally—on blackboards propped against the wall and modest shops trading first and foremost with the locals, not the holidaymakers. It also has a splendid museum and library housed in what must be the ugliest building for miles around—with immaculate classical 'Burton's' a stone's throw away!

It has trams and a ferry (which gave one local resident, working in the bank at Knott End the distinction of being possibly the only person in Britain going to work on a tram and a boat!). Not only does Fleetwood have trams—and the only remaining true street-tramway in Britain—it uses them, and is used to them. They approach the town down the middle of a kind of dual carriageway (giving this essentially 'Lancashire' town an air of the Netherlands) then run slap-bang down the main shopping street. Eccentrically, the council permits parking in the street, with not *quite* enough room for traffic to pass a stationary tram. This safeguards boarding passengers and surprises drivers used to the inevitable contemporary priority for his little tin box. Occasionally, a delivery driver, unused to the ways of the town will double park; along will come a tram and everything *stops*. No one seems to mind—such is the (welcome) eccentricity of the place.

Homegoing workpeople, housewives, schoolchildren— everybody—uses the tram naturally, joining the holidaymakers coming in from Blackpool for the ride over the cliffs or to the market. At one time they were the cross-bench cars of the private Blackpool & Fleetwood Company, then the splendid Pullman-like cars of the early Blackpool Corporation days, then the huge

'Balloon' double deckers of the inter-war years. Now the trendy one-person operated Jubilee makes its stately way along Lord Street to turn round the loop. It makes little difference to the car driver faced with a surprising sight bearing down on him round the wrong side of, of all things, a lighthouse in the middle of the road!

One of the two lighthouses by
Decimus Burton at Fleetwood

6 Mid-Victorian Blackpool

'The months of September and October are considered the genteel season', but the sea still threatens

The Preston & Wyre Railway, together with the Manchester & Bolton and the Bolton & Preston, ran excursions to Fleetwood in 1844 and was the first railway to do so. In that summer 60,000 people travelled at half fare in open wagons to enjoy the sea-air. Not all of them would have gone through to Fleetwood; a fair proportion would have left the trains at Kirkham for Lytham and Poulton for Blackpool and the railway company saw the sense of building branch lines to the two resorts.

In the summer of 1846 Thomas Cook of Leicester ran his first excursion to Scotland by way of Fleetwood and the sea route and it was such a success that he organised another the following year; by the time Queen Victoria, Prince Albert, the Prince of Wales and Princess Royal landed at Fleetwood on their way back from Scotland (the first time, incidentally, that the Queen had set foot in her Royal Duchy of Lancaster) both the branch lines were coming to the end of their first successful summer seasons.

But the railway, like Hesketh Fleetwood himself, was in financial difficulties; the company brought in a prominent banker, Clement Royds of Rochdale (a man important enough to influence the naming of his local church 'St Clements'!) to put the line into order. Railway amalgamations were in the air, the Manchester & Leeds joined up with, amongst others, the Manchester & Bolton and became the Lancashire & Yorkshire Railway (the North's own railway) and the Preston & Wyre became jointly owned by this and the London & North Western Railway in 1849.

A visitor, arriving at Blackpool's new station 'though very large and lofty' was 'very uncomfortably crowded with spectators . . . and idle people of all sorts and sizes'. He had been to Blackpool before—as a young man in 1809—and presumably remembered the days when all visitors were part of the 'big house party' at the resort. The railway had changed all that, bringing trippers in their thousands; it had taken him eight hours in a coach from Preston then—now it took less than two from the far side of Lancashire.

All restrictions were now removed from building. The railway linked the Fylde with the world outside and that world was Blackpool's oyster. By 1851 it had a resident population of 2,000 which could swell to double that in the summer—plus the trippers. All the same it had little or no provision for sanitation or the supply of fresh water: 'some houses require privys', a letter from a South Shore resident said in 1847, 'and many bedrooms are open to the shippons. Can you do anything to compel the regular whitewashing of the houses quarterly and the manure placed at least ten yards from the door in proper places. I am sure that cleanliness would do much to raise the moral condition of the poor.'

The *Lancashire Directory* of 1851 took a more optimistic line:

None here need complain of lassitude or ennui—there is amusement and employment for all. The horseman, pedestrian the geologist, the conchologist and zoologist may ever find occupation on the shore and the herbalist on the land . . . The laying out of streets and walks, the erection of handsome houses and shops on every side, the establishment of elegant hotels and billiards, news and coffee rooms, lounges, bazaars etc . . . and the opening and enlargement of places of worship, bespeak the rising importance of the town and the anxiety of the inhabitants to render the sojourn of their visitors pleasant and comfortable . . . The months of September and October are considered the genteel season.

The same year the Layton-with-Warbreck (still no 'Blackpool') Board of Health was formed, a 'Blackpool Improvement Act' was passed by Parliament in 1853, and by 1857 the *Directory and Gazetteer* was able to report:

Great praise, we are glad to say, is due to the Commissioners of Blackpool who have done all in their power to sewer the town and cleanse it from all impurities, so that the most refined visitor may be pleased with its purity and sweetness.

The Commissioners built a gas works, a Fylde Waterworks Company was registered and the town grew and grew. By 1861 Layton-with-Warbreck was home for nearly 4,000 people. A second railway line was built—from Blackpool to Lytham but not connected to the existing lines; all the same, 35,000 people used the line in its first three months.

The first pier (the present North Pier) was built in 1863 and the first piped water supply was laid on in the following year. Fine hotels (and a few splendid private villas) lined the sea-front and plans were revealed to develop the area north of Talbot Square as a private estate of houses and hotels to be called Claremont Park. It was an 'exclusive' district and visitors were required to pay a toll of one penny to use the road which linked Talbot Square to the Gynn. They preferred to pay rather than use the treacherous path along the crumbling cliffs. The grand Imperial Hotel, by far the biggest and most splendid yet, opened on this new promenade in 1867. Even today there is a subtle change of atmosphere as one moves north from Talbot Square and a decidedly stylish air about the buildings and gardens.

Beyond the Gynn Uncle Tom's Cabin provided a sharp contrast to the refinement and proper decorum of Claremont Park. It had developed haphazardly (as these things seem to do) from a refreshment stall established near the gypsies then camped on the cliffs; it developed an open-air 'dancing stage', rudimentary pavilion, hobby horses, photographers and even a camera obscura. The proprietor, aware of the popularity of Harriet Beecher Stowe's novel, placed wooden figures of the main characters atop the building and gave it the name 'Uncle Tom's Cabin'. The rendezvous was extremely popular despite (or because of) its dubious reputation.

The sea—Blackpool's permanent adversary as well as its raison d'être—crunched away at the cliffs below Uncle Tom's Cabin and the Imperial alike—and at the low-lying promenade to the south. Time after time the sea showed the town who was master and in 1865 the Local Board was empowered to improve and extend the sea-front and erect sea defences. Even during the construction of the grand new promenade the sea struck; in 1868 and again the following year there were tremendous storms. The North Pier was damaged, the promenade and sea defence works almost destroyed, hotels flooded to a depth of several feet. Lamp-posts were uprooted, one house was ripped open by the force of the waves and shingle was thrown up, waist high against others.

By April, 1870, the new promenade was ready for its official opening. It had a carriageway over 30ft wide, an impressive twenty-five foot asphalt parade and a solid granite-sett slope leading down to the beach. 'In brilliant weather', the *Preston Pilot* reported, 'a grand procession, with not less than twelve Lancashire Mayors, gentry, tradesmen, schoolchildren, benefit societies, volunteers and military bands made for Talbot Square where the official opening took place . . . During the evening a grand ball was held and the town was illuminated in honour of the occasion.'

The Illuminations are generally acknowledged as having begun in 1912—but should this brief reference be taken as proof that they began forty years before?

In February 1871, with the new sea-defences only a few months old newspaper reports began to appear of further storm damage, just like the old days before the new promenade was built. A correspondent in the *Preston Pilot* refuted the claims. '. . . it is a gross exaggeration in every respect. The total amount of damage to the three miles of sea fencing is less than £10.'

All the same, the sea fought a constant battle with the towns along the coast. The cliffs to the north of Blackpool were crumbling away at an alarming rate—yards a year. The legends that occur in many seaside places about lost villages under the waves were fact so far as the Fylde was concerned. The mysterious Roman Portus Setantii of which no trace has ever been reliably found is assumed to have been off the coast at Fleetwood and the village of Singleton Thorpe almost certainly stood a good mile west of the present coastline at Norbreck.

The Reverend William Thornber, wrote a history of the Blackpool area in 1837 and stated quite categorically that the village was destroyed by a great storm in 1554. He went on to say that the villagers moved inland and built the present Singleton—which tends to destroy his story; Singleton itself is an old settlement which obviously existed long before the mid-sixteenth century. All the same, exploration of the sands far out from the cliffs in 1886 discovered the remains of walling which could have been cottages.

A good half mile out from the coast at Bispham is Pennystone Rock where it is said 'there existed a small roadside inn, celebrated far and wide for its strong ale and whilst the thirsty traveller was refreshing himself within . . . his horse was tethered to an iron ring fixed to this stone'. The Inn disappeared but the stone remained, glimpsed from time to time at extreme low-water.

Lytham, too, suffered from the sea. Sometimes the storms would gnaw away at the sandhills, sometimes huge banks of shingle ('stanners') would build up at a ferocious pace. Lytham Lighthouse was built on the Double Stanner Bank in 1847 but washed away in 1863. On the south side of the estuary, the Ribble channel ran near to the coast—and a channel of sorts existed into the present century. Then the channel suddenly dried up, then reappeared much nearer the shore and much shallower.

The rivers have played their part in altering the lines of this coast. The western rivers of Lancashire rise in the gritstone Pennines— hills composed of a soft sandstone (artificially ground to a fine sand, then reconstituted into something like drawing chalk; blocks of it have been used to 'stone' generations of Lancashire doorsteps!). Brought down by rivers which tend to be swift-flowing, the sand is swept out to sea and returned by the incoming tide. The prevailing south-westerlies dry the sand rapidly and sweep it inland. It is a fine sand which builds up quickly (one can virtually see the sandhills forming in a strong gale). Hence the advice to the ladies of Southport to wear veils at all times!

What the rivers took from the Pennines and the sea from the cliffs north of Blackpool was given back to the Ribble estuary and the coast between it and Formby. Even the Mersey dredgers and the restriction of the Ribble between walls (to improve navigation to Preston) have affected the issue. The dredgers have dumped millions of tons of silt out in Liverpool Bay, and the Ribble channel, by speeding the flow of water down from Preston, has swept sand out to sea which would have spread inside the estuary.

The coast has been a shifting, almost 'live' thing. Speed's map of 1610 shows the coastline north and south of the Ribble to have been concave—two wide bays backed by huge 'mosses'. Now both sections of coast are convex; the river Alt, south of Formby point was a substantial port with a good channel to the sea. The Mersey had to cut across this channel, and eventually did, forcing the sand back against the coast and filling up the channel.

The sea left Southport, but not, apparently for the first time; the inrush which brought the high tides to the then new sea wall in the 1830s was only a cycle in the great shiftings of the coastline. Kilgrymoles, one of the legendary villages, was supposed to have stood off the coast to the north of the Ribble estuary. It could well have been destroyed by the sea which formed the northern 'bay' in front of Marton Moss. Later changes produced the area called, evocatively, Blowing Sands and the wide, smooth curve reaching round from Lytham to Blackpool. The sand—fine white quartz from the Pennines—built up, the stanners shifted, the tough marram grass grew and the land stabilised.

Across this land the new railway from Lytham to Blackpool was built, easily and swiftly. There was only one intermediate station at South Shore near the Blackpool end. For 6 miles the trains ran between the sandhills with only the birds for company and only the occasional cottage to break the scene. This area, Cross Slack, seemed somehow sheltered from the vicious westerly gales and the cold wind from the north. If it could be developed in a suitable way it could provide the Fylde with yet another resort.

These were the 1870s—the pinnacle years of Victorian splendour and achievement. The country (if not all the people in it) was as wealthy, as confident as it had ever been. Lancashire had built, not Jerusalem among its dark satanic mills, but a vast trading empire that made the British Empire possible. It had coal, cotton, and engineering. It built the engines that used the coal to drive the machinery that wove the cloth; the cloth was taken on its railways, hauled by its locomotives to its ports, loaded on to its ships (driven by its coal) to all the corners of the world. Then its ships brought raw materials of a more exotic kind back. Britannia might rule the waves, but the Northern businessmen had a lot to do with what sailed on them!

The sun and the clean air of the seaside beckoned. The better-off had moved up socially and had moved up physically, out of the smoke-strangled towns into villas and demi-palaces on the hills around. But they still had to look down on the belching chimneys. The green leaves of spring turned black in a week and flowers were stunted and shrivelled by the soot and grey, smoke-shrouded sky. Yet only a few miles away, on the coast, the air sparkled it seemed, like the clean bright sea. Flowers grew and lace-curtains stayed white. During a brief holiday at the seaside, with 'th' mill' and all its problems seemingly a thousand light years away it was possible to imagine living in this paradise. The railway could transport you to the seaside in little more than an hour; therefore it could transport you to the weaving shed and foundry shop in the same length of time.

The staircase of Blackpool's Casino, designed by Joseph Emberton in 1936

The Seafield Hotel in Blackpool—Victorian-built but given an Art Deco frontage in 1936

Splendid Art Deco hotels, built in 1937, in Cleveleys

A Jubilee tram at Blackpool's
Pleasure Beach

The narrow-gauge railway (it used to be a tramway) on the pier at Southport. The
lake below was constructed later

7 St Annes-on-the-Sea

Enterprise and expertise. A garden city, majestic and melodic

With the benefit of hindsight it is easy to see that the kind of development attempted at Fleetwood by Hesketh Fleetwood and Decimus Burton came too early. An efficient transport network was still in the making; more importantly the social order, although changing, had not yet 'broadened' sufficiently—modest wealth had not yet filtered down to the new business class.

The project which turned the sandhills and stanners of Cross Slack into the gracious oasis of St Annes-on-the-Sea was better timed and the location better suited. Wealth had not only increased as a result of industry, it had spread—like a growing plant, upwards and outwards—to a comparatively large number of families, rather than permeating downwards generation by generation.

Individual enterprise there certainly was (the individual hand-loom weaver of the 1820s could find himself the owner of a substantial mill by the 1860s) and, in the cotton textile industry particularly, the joint stock company was common. The in-dustrialised sector of the North of England developed unaided—therefore unfettered by the kind of interest Hesketh Fleetwood represented. Most of its most successful men came from 'ordinary' families and the image of the rough-hewn self-made man is not too far from the truth.

The divisions were particularly apparent in Lancashire. Industry inhabited the east and south-east, the west and south-west were agricultural and manorial. Historically, the east had been under-developed, the west (for all its marshes and shifting coast) enjoyed a modest prosperity. The east was predominantly Parliamentarian and Presbyterian during the Civil War, its few substantial landowners supporting the Roundheads, the west, Protestant and Catholic, upheld the Royalist cause.

Historically, again, it had been 'Catholic Lancashire' for generations. The burgeoning of industry brought other people into the east and south-east—people who were new, adaptable, non-Catholic. The new towns and expanding villages of the Pennines were a fertile proving ground for men like Wesley and the indomitable preacher William Grimshaw. They, and their ideas, were part and parcel of the new social order developing in the prolific east and south-east.

The new order of the Industrial Society was a complex mixture—radicalism, the Co-operative movement, grass-roots education, self-help and the all-pervading Nonconformist religion—totally alien to the traditional order of things. The society was self-made, its manners and mores formed by and dictated by itself alone. It was wealthy, in some cases ostentatiously so, and it expressed its wealth through its town halls rather than its country houses—and its mills, its equivalent of the medieval abbeys. Mills and gigantic railway stations, both elaborately ornamented, were the biggest buildings built since the Reformation. In a way they represented just *that*—the dominance of the protestant-industrial-Anglo-Saxon ethic.

Irish Catholic immigrant labour might have built the canals and railways but Church of England, Methodist, Congregational and Unitarian and all the others who looked away from Rome owned them and benefited from them. 'Commercial Conservatism' was apparent, but Liberalism dominated.

Yet it was something of a ghetto mentality. For all its affluence, the North was 'outside'—not fighting against the tide but running faster than the mainstream. It felt ill at ease in the South, more at home in the United States or Germany. It developed the kind of arrogance normal in such circumstances. It is said that a northern businessman, sensing that the under-manager at a famous and exclusive London hotel was being condescending stood quietly, awaiting his chance. When the under-manager enquired, 'Would Sir take the lift or would he feel safer using the stairs?', the businessman switched to broad Lancashire and bellowed, 'Nay Lad! Ah'll be awreet i'th'Hoist!' if the story is true—and it could very well be—the man's wife would have given him the 'ticking off'

St George's Square, St Annes

of a lifetime, once the door to the exclusive suite was firmly closed. The women took the society and moulded it, elaborating it to the extravagancies of wedding-cake icing!

So, even if the northern businessman had been offered a Decimus Burton house at Fleetwood he would most likely have declined it, preferring his money to go to his own kind. If for no other reason, the success of St Annes-on-the-Sea was assured; it was the latest example of the North building the North.

During a visit to the Fylde Coast in the summer of 1874, Elijah Hargreaves, a successful businessman from the Rossendale valley in East Lancashire made the acquaintance of Thomas Fair, Agent for the Clifton Estate at Lytham. He had already explored the vast stretch of sandhills between Lytham and Blackpool and could sense the advantage of development. Much to his surprise, he found Fair had already done some preliminary work on a plan for a new 'town' on the dunes. Together they formulated the plans that were to result in St Annes.

To raise the capital for the development company, Hargreaves went to his friends, the businessmen of Haslingden and Rossendale;

71

(in exactly the same way, a decade later, Holroyd Smith went to his friends in Halifax for finance for the Blackpool Tramway). These canny northern businessmen preferred to put their money where they could see it! A company, the St Anne's-on-the-Sea Land and Building Company Limited, was registered, John Talbot Clifton granted it a lease of 1,100 years on the land and Clifton himself cut the first sod and laid the first stone on 31 March 1875.

The generally accepted story is that the first structure was a church dedicated to St Anne, but Porter's *History of the Fylde* written barely a year after the stone-laying, gives a different version. Writing of the 'embryo town' Porter says:

> The whole of the land of St Annes-on-the-Sea was leased to a company of gentlemen for a term of 1,100 years by John Talbot Clifton Esq., and on the 31st of March 1875 the formality of laying the first stone of the future watering-place was gone through by Master John T. Clifton, the eldest son of T. H. Clifton Esq., M.P. The ceremony was accomplished amidst a large concourse of people and was, in fact, the commencement of the handsome and commodious hotel near to the railway station, which has since been completed.

There are two variations to the generally accepted version. According to Porter the young John Clifton laid the stone, not John Talbot Clifton, and it was the foundation stone of the St Annes Hotel! Porter may be wrong, the stone-laying may have been for the church, or there may have been two ceremonies, one for the church and one for the hotel on the same day, but as Porter was writing so soon after the event one is inclined to accept his version. Certainly, there was a station by this time. 'Cross Slack' station was opened in November 1873 and re-named 'St Annes' in January 1875.

Maxwell and Tuke, architects from Bury (again, keeping the enterprise local to East Lancashire), were retained by the company to (as Porter says) 'judiciously and tastefully arrange' the town 'intersected by broad streets with gentle curves'. Maxwell and Tuke were to go on to design Blackpool Tower later.

Porter's account continues:

> The houses are intended to be built either singly or in pairs with few exceptions, but in no case will any group comprise more than six; gardens in each instance are to front the dwellings. A promenade, 3,000

feet in length and 180 feet in width, has been formed with asphalt along the marine aspect, and already between twenty and thirty villas have been raised on the sides of the recently made thoroughfares. A public garden with conservatories is also in course of formation, as well as efficient gasworks and other requisites.

One of the men who stamped his personality indelibly on the infant St Annes was William J. Porritt of Helmshore, Haslingden. He spent £250,000 (profits from his Sunnybank Mill in Helmshore) in building houses in the town. Besides the mill he also owned quarries at Hasseldon and Torside, in Rossendale, and he used this stone to build some of the finest houses of the period.

'Victorian' architecture conjures up images of excess, pastiche and ostentation for ostentation's sake. Porritt's houses are finely proportioned, restrained and commendably 'original'. Details, even down to carving on the mini-capitals flanking the front doors are identical, running counter to the usual Victorian practice of individually designed dwellings and variations within a theme. His Rossendale stone is remarkably 'pure' (stone from Pennine quarries further east tends to incorporate patches of iron-ore) and this is complemented by end walls in a yellow 'London Stock' type brick with darker brick 'strapping'—a modest elaboration used to great effect. Roofs are suitably steeply-pitched, gables decoratively (but again modestly) barge-boarded, ridges topped with perforated terra-cotta tiles. A pale green slate is used, and each house carries the 'Porritt Mark'— a diamond in darker slate.

The effect of these houses—scores of them—is delightful. Victorians were fond of 'gothic' and 'classic' divisions; these are neither, yet they are not lacking in style. They state their purpose admirably—houses for the moderately well-to-do which are meant for living in, comfortably and conveniently. The stables and carriage houses in the mews at the back are moderately sized and have the appearance of the modern garage; these are not the massive stable-blocks of the upper class, but accommodations for the carriage that every middlingly wealthy man owned (or aspired to!).

'Gentle curves' of Porritt houses were built, and straight lines on both sides of the main road through the town. The one-time St Annes-on-the-Sea town hall is 'Porritt', as is the Conservative

Club. The section of St Annes built by Porritt is a highly successful example of what the practical Victorian architect and entrepreneur could do when the partnership was harmonious (they are, after all, 'speculative development') without the aid of the devotee of the Arts and Crafts or any other movement. That makes them all the more remarkable. Yet they remain virtually unknown to the architectural *cognoscenti*.

Within ten years of the start of building, St Annes was large enough to contemplate a Pier. A suitably modest one was opened by Lord Stanley in 1885 and a pavilion (in a style which can only be called 'Moorish Fantasic') was added in 1899. A Floral Hall completed the complex in 1910. The Pier was one of St Annes' most select rendezvous from the start, and remained so. In its later years it was graced by the 'definitive' Pier Orchestra under the baton of one Lionel Johns—of the Halle Orchestra, no less. A large sepia photograph of the maestro adorned the pierhead entrance—raven haired and classically profiled he looked suitably solemn and refined. The photograph stayed the same although Lionel Johns aged to silver-locked distinction! The Pier was also home for a repertory company of 'suitable' status whose productions always had the same 'background music' of the sea swishing about beneath the theatre!

The Pier suffered the fate of so many—decline in popularity, a massive fire, threats of demolition, attempts at up-dating. The memories are harder to extinguish than the fire—potted palms, the tinkle of tea-cups, metal tea pots with hot, difficult-to-handle handles, wicker chairs, glass topped tables with doilies beneath, the sound of the sea joining the strains of a selection from *Maritana* and a vague aroma of hot steam and damp woodwork.

Gardens—of a vaguely alpine kind—appeared on the Promenade. Water played an important part in the effect, as did the white 'limestone' of decorative bridges and rockeries made whiter by the huge white light of the seaside. The 'folk art' of decorative work in sea-shore pebbles is used to great effect, even forming paving in some places. This kind of decoration is common all along the Fylde Coast but reaches its pinnacle of perfection in the sea-front gardens at St Annes. For all that it was a Victorian foundation

The pier at St Annes

(and concept) St Annes is Edwardian—graceful, 'settled' to the point of complaceny. The early stone gave way to brick and terra-cotta, larger houses expressing something other than the pioneering spirit of the Porritt homes. Wealth was greater and a more monied class was settling at the sea-side. Gradually, St Annes spread towards Lytham. 'Ansdell' (a name which associates itself in the mind with 'St Annes' and 'Ainsdale') developed between the two, then formed the link with both. The town 'strolled' (rather than spread) round the curve of the coast.

If the incoming residents left grim bethel-like nonconformist chapels behind them in the mill towns they found splendid evocations of each particular denomination in the sea-side town

75

that were—whisper the words—positively *Church of England* like. The 'Marble Church' at Fairhaven could be High Anglican or even Roman Catholic; it is in fact Congregational. It is also not *quite* marble, but clear white faience and a spectacular achievement for the Art Nouveau movement. It is totally unexpected—consummate and again, virtually unknown.

St Annes' biggest hotel was *very* big. It began as the Imperial Hydro, but changed its name to the far more suitable 'Majestic'. And so it was, right down to Geraldo and his Broadcasting Orchestra playing in its ballroom. Its majesty is no more and luxury flats rise in its place. Anywhere else they would be extremely well designed, but the splendour of the Majestic seems to haunt them.

The town developed, growing greener and lusher with each succeeding spring. The leisurely pace quickened to swinging the occasional golf club and in the course of time golf became a staple industry. There were no less than four courses, each with a precise position within the overall area: St Annes Old Links at the Blackpool end, Green Drive at the Lytham, Fairhaven on the other side of Lytham Park and, bang in the centre, in every sense of the word, the renowned Royal Lytham & St Annes. HM Land Registry may be pushed to one end of Lytham Promenade, Premium Bonds and the Football League may have their headquarters in the town, but the Royal Lytham & St Annes sets the style. Yet it does not dominate the town (as golf dominates St Andrews); it is Royal but not Ancient. The town also takes quiet satisfaction in the knowledge the Blackpool Airport is in St Annes!

The links with Blackpool were inevitable, but one has the feeling they were formed for convenience, not necessity; there is still a symbolic stretch of open country between the two, even on the sand-drifted coast road. There is no such break between Blackpool and its northern neighbour, Cleveleys.

Inevitable, too, was the eventual amalgamation of Lytham with St Annes. Its first joint Council, elected in 1927 contrasts sharply with the 'grocer-brick-maker' image presented by that year's Mayor of Blackpool. The Mayor of the Borough of Lytham St Annes was an architect and surveyor, an immigrant from the Pennine foothills in 1890, when St Annes was struggling out of its infancy. There were two other architects on the council, a solicitor, an estate agent, a 'contractor', a professor of music, four 'cotton manufacturers' or 'directors', four described as 'gentleman' and five who could be vaguely described as being 'in trade'—and one of those was an undertaker. There were also two women; neither is ascribed a profession or any qualification.

The new borough was a sizeable one, in area at least. Blackpool has long boasted of its coastline ('Seven Golden Miles') but Lytham St Annes' is almost as long, curving round from the open sea to the 'southern aspect' or Lytham Green. Clearly, it could be, indeed *is*, a complete resort in itself. It had two piers, the frolicsome delights of an open air swimming pool, one of the prerequisites of every holiday paradise in the thirties, a huge marine boating lake at Fairhaven (surely designed to link the two ends together?), the stark simplicity of the greensward at Lytham with its sentinel windmill and a quiet relaxed atmosphere which was less soporific than Southport, less frenetic than Blackpool.

It also had, and has, a green aspect that made Lytham 'Leafy Lytham' generations ago. Less predictable is St Annes' mature landscape. Ashton Gardens, sheltering behind the sea-front buildings are barely seventy years old, yet the tree-scapes are full-bodied and merely breeze-stirred, the roses prolific, their perfume almost alcoholic. The inscription in the rose garden is a familiar one—simple, direct, and a gentle reminder that could apply to the town as well as the garden: 'One is Nearer God's Heart in a Garden than anywhere else on Earth.' It needn't be said, but in St Annes, it *is*.

The town kept its balance between resident and visitor. The shops in the wide main street leading from the station to St Annes pier reflect the stable values of the town—quality and style (rather than mere fashion). There is a bank that would not look out of place in a West Country market town, a Tudor building, and a solid 'Lutyenesque cenotaph'. The small cafés and snack bars are in the side streets. The visitor will look in vain for the familiar pub-sign. After the St Annes Hotel, the founding fathers built none; the respectable nonconformist early resident would not need them and the visitor could find them elsewhere if he wished.

Lytham has its own shopping centre—a village of butchers,

newsagents, greengrocers and dress-shops, with the casual informality of shopping that goes with a village. Less a resort than St Annes it has its pubs (or rather inns) and, perhaps oddly in the circumstances, a less uncompromising aspect than its newer sister along the road. Even today, the contrast between Victorian conformity and the carefree Regency is apparent.

Increasingly, the resident predominates. In Lytham it is the affluent who can afford to live there, in St Annes the army of the retired. The Porritt houses divide conveniently into rest homes, providing much more than the bare essentials for living past sixty. The retirement bungalows, too, fan out across the countryside; the goal for many a Lancastrian is a modest home in this sunlit gentle town where the pace is easy, the hills infinitesimal. Yet many return to their old haunts; the sun may shine, the gardens bloom, but they find it difficult to put down roots in the fine sand of the coast.

8 The Blackpool Trams I

'The movement of the car was everything that could be desired'

Tramways and Blackpool are irrevocably linked. It ran the first electric street tramway in the country and it runs the last, one of the most modern in the world. The story of the trams is almost the story of the town itself—developing, changing, expanding and contracting as the situation demands, modernising and innovating; above all *surviving* in a changing world.

By the early 1880s the 'watering places' had given way to the holiday resort. In these expanding Victorian days, business was booming. Blackpool had a 2-mile long promenade; it had electric street lighting (a pioneer system); it had been a Borough since 1876; its population was well over 14,000 and looked like doubling in the next decade or so. It needed a more efficient public transport system and that meant trams.

Trams, horse-drawn and steam-driven, were running in many towns up and down the country. (There had been a proposal for a coastal steam tramway the year after Blackpool became a Borough.) There were even electric tramways, notably between Portrush and the Giants Causeway in Northern Ireland and along the sea-front at Brighton.

Blackpool, which had been discussing some form of tramway for ten years set up a committee to investigate. They dismissed Volk's Electric Railway at Brighton as 'little more than a toy' and the coaches on the Giant's Causeway line as 'great blundering, thundering things'. It looked as though Blackpool might have to settle for the diminutive horse trams like they had in the rival Douglas or the steam cars, as blundering and thundering as anything else that was churning through the streets of Rochdale, Birmingham and scores of other smoky towns and cities.

Yet there was already an electric tramway right under their

noses; toy-like and unsuccessful perhaps, but running in the grounds of the Winter Gardens just a few yards from the Promenade and introduced as an attraction for that summer of 1884. It is not surprising that they were in ignorance of it. It ran, after a fashion, for a few days in July and was then closed down.

In August, a Mr Michael Holroyd Smith of Halifax arrived at the Winter Gardens to try to get the line working again. He had already built a narrow-gauge line in the garden of a fellow Halifax engineer and, importantly, a standard-gauge line outside his factory in Manchester. He approached the Tramway Committee with a possible answer to their problem. First he took them to see the rejuvenated Winter Gardens line, then to see his standard-gauge line in Manchester.

It convinced the Committee. Delightedly, they reported:

> The movement of the car was everything that could be desired. Commencing with an almost imperceptible motion free from the last jerk, it gradually increased in velocity until the maximum speed was obtained, when it was brought to a standstill again, either gradually, without the least jerk, or suddenly, within a distance equal to its own car length.

The report reveals the same pleasure (the same wonderment almost) that Fanny Burney felt when she travelled on the Liverpool & Manchester Railway sixty years before.

The decision was made almost immediately. Holroyd Smith's system would be adopted—standard-gauge and a conduit system, taking the current from a slot between the running rails—and Holroyd Smith set about obtaining financial backing. Much of this came from his home town; Halifax was one of the most well-to-do towns in the country at the time. Not without reason do they say the Lancashireman saves for the joy of spending whereas the Yorkshireman saves for the joy of saving! Halifax, after all, had and still has the biggest building society in the world and although its hills are steep the money never rolls down them and into the river!

Of the ten directors of the Blackpool Electric Tramway Company formed in January 1885 six were from Halifax or the neighbouring Brighouse; from Blackpool came Councillors Bickerstaffe and Broadbent. The Secretary of the Company was the

Borough Treasurer! The Company was offered £20,000 more than the £30,000 nominal it needed. Lancashire and Yorkshire businessmen knew their stuff whether it was cotton or wool or trams; the red and white roses grew from the same stem when it came to *brass*!

The first rail was laid on 13 March and the whole 2-mile line was completed and operating by the end of September—a remarkable achievement by any standards. The electric trams weren't cheap (a ticket cost twice as much as the horse bus) nor were they particularly fast, but they provided a smoother, more comfortable ride and were enormously popular.

They were not, however, entirely trouble-free. Power transmission itself was at the pioneering stage still, generators were inefficient and the conduit caused problems; a broken collector shoe, a sudden flurry of sand sweeping down into the slot between the rails, and the whole system ground to a halt. Occasionally the tramway had to use horse-traction (to the amusement, no doubt, of the rival horse-bus drivers). All the same, the tramway developed— a new power station, new extension down Lytham road, parallel to the Promenade, then a relief loop to join the Lytham road line to the sea-front by the Victoria Pier. The trams of the Lytham St Annes undertaking started running through along a new line linked to the Lytham road track. They had no problems with conduit or power failure, they were *gas* driven.

Expanding traffic meant new tramcars. The short four-wheelers of 1885 gave way to the 'Lancasters' of 1894—huge bogied cars so big they wouldn't fit into the depot. The local bus owners howled angrily that they were dangerous but the *Blackpool Herald* insisted that, 'the big car is unquestionably the car of the future so far as Blackpool is concerned'.

By 1897 it was obvious that the big tramcar might represent the future but the conduit system did not. Temperamental and expensive, it had broken the hearts of drivers and Committee chairmen alike; after the resignation of one Tramways Committee chairman no one could be found to fill the post. Not for nothing was it called 'the Committee of Tribulation'.

In 1896 Blackpool had acquired a new Electrical Engineer, R. C.

Quin, for its tramway. In August 1897 he suggested to the Tramways Committee that the whole conduit system should be abandoned and converted to overhead collection, in time for the 1898 season! The Committee accepted his recommendation (no doubt with a heartfelt sigh of relief) and prepared for the end of the conduit and the beginning of a better, happier world.

They counted without the opposition of a certain Dr Hardman, consistent critic of the Corporation and the intransigence of the Board of Trade. Notwithstanding the fact that current collection from overhead wires was commonplace on the Continent and in the USA, there was an extremely influential body of opinion that objected to it for various reasons: the wires could snap in a strong wind, the wires could pull down the supporting poles, and so on. There were even aesthetic arguments—'wires in the sky' were ugly; London suburbs had trolley collection, but the parts of the central area which had trams kept to the unwieldy and expensive conduit right up to the abandonment in the 1950s. (If a tram was to run through from a suburb to a conduit area it had to change from one system to another, a time-consuming and expensive business.)

It looked as though Blackpool was stuck with its conduit (although the Board of Trade, in its wisdom, suggested they should adopt battery traction, even more temperamental, expensive and inefficient than the conduit). Eventually, the Board of Trade relented and the long awaited conversion started. But in the meantime more new trams arrived, the biggest ever, carrying eighty-six people and built on an entirely new principle. The entrance spread across the whole of the end of the car, the doorway was to the bottom in the centre by the driver, and there were *two* flanking staircases to reach the upper deck.

Inevitably, perhaps, they were christened 'Dreadnoughts' and they ran until 1934 when, no doubt to their amazement, they found themselves running alongside their descendants—equally large but curiously bulbous—'streamliners' which were not like any tram before them, as the Dreadnoughts had been unlike their predecessors. One Dreadnought, mercifully, was saved, restored and still runs.

Curiously, all the time the Board of Trade was blocking

Blackpool Corporation's move to scrap the conduit, the overhead was going up all the way from Talbot Road station to Fleetwood, an illogicality no doubt noted by the Tramways Committee. Construction of the Blackpool & Fleetwood Tramroad had begun in July 1897 and by June 1898 experimental runs were taking place. Officially this was a 'tramroad', defined as being 'a tramway laid elsewhere than along a street or road'. Admittedly, for most of its length it was on a separate track but at both ends it ran along what were undoubtedly streets and roads—and one end was in Blackpool, 'wires in the sky' and all! One can only guess at the words used to describe the equivocating Board of Trade 'down there in London' and the troublesome Dr Hardman nearer home!

The delay in converting the Blackpool street-tramways to overhead collection gave the Councillors an opportunity to sample the Blackpool to Fleetwood run, and any doubts could surely have been dispelled. The long sleek bogied single-deckers cracked along at 30mph separate, for most of the way, from other traffic. The first trams delivered were open sided, but soon there would be saloons, perhaps even trailers. The contrast between this and the ageing Blackpool system was obvious; the Councillors could, however, console themselves with the thought that shortly they too would have overhead collection, even if the separating of tram tracks from other traffic would have to wait.

9 The Blackpool Trams II

Conversion and expansion. Acquisition and 'arrangement'

Converted to overhead collection and with more new trams, the Blackpool tramway system flourished. The profits for 1899 were £7,500, for 1900 £13,500. An extension north (along the new section of Promenade) met (but did not link with) the Fleetwood Tramroad at the Gynn. Two tramroutes serving the residential parts of the town were opened: by way of Marton to Waterloo Road, a Central station and Lytham road route in 1901 and a north-east to Layton route the following year.

In ten years Blackpool's population had doubled, and more than tripled since the trams started running in 1885. The 1901 Census showed that 47,348 people lived in Blackpool. There were plans afoot to widen the main sea-front promenade between Talbot Square and South Shore to provide an 80ft wide roadway with the trams running on their own paved reservation on the seaward side and a further pedestrian parade between it and the beach.

By 1905 it was finished and the main Promenade took on the appearance it has today. The gaudy Golden Mile was yet to come but the Tower was there, along with the Palace Theatre, the Great Wheel, the Palatine Hotel, the Royal, the County, the Clifton, Manchester, Queen's and a score of other hotels, a thousand other boarding houses.

It was possible to travel all the way from East Beach, Lytham to Fleetwood by tram, then take a vessel of the Isle of Man Steam Packet Company to Douglas, then a horse tram to Derby Castle and an electric one up the coast to Ramsey (or up the mountain to the summit of Snaefell.) Then there was the proposal to extend the Lytham tramway and join it up to that of Southport by way of a Transporter Bridge across the Ribble!

Alternatively, visitors to the Fylde Coast could travel to

Lord Street, Southport

The Royal Clifton Hotel on Southport's Promenade

Blackpool Tower, intended to rival Paris' landmark, was officially opened in 1894

Fleetwood by tram, take the ferry to Knott End, then by horse charabanc to the (then) terminus of the Garstang & Knott End Railway at Pilling. In 1904, indeed, the Blackpool & Fleetwood Tramroad formed a new company to operate motor charabancs over the route and later that service was extended as far as Lancaster and Morecambe.

But the motor bus was in its infancy; the motor car was a rich man's toy. The tram reigned supreme and the tramways were a gold mine. In the last glorious summer before World War I the Tramroad Company alone carried 3.6 million passengers and made a profit of £21,000.

The only competitor was the railway (in most places it was the tram competing with the railway rather than the other way round). The Blackpool & Fleetwood line had competition from the Lancashire & Yorkshire Railway from the start. Before the arrival of the coastal tramway the railway had had a monopoly on traffic between Blackpool and Fleetwood but it was an awkward time-consuming journey for the passengers. Trains ran out from Talbot Square (North) Station to Poulton where they reversed for the 6-mile run up to Fleetwood; shortly after the opening of the tramroad the railway built a connecting curve at Poulton so that trains could run direct. They put on extra trains, cut the journey time to 15 minutes and cut the fare from 9d to 6d, the same fare as the tram which took at least three times as long.

The tramway survived the competition. It did not rely on through traffic and the estates along the line were expanding rapidly. The only cloud on the horizon was the problem of the lease, granted when the tramroad opened in 1898 and due for renewal in 1919. Blackpool had made it clear that it would not be willing to renew the Company's rights within the Borough and with the absorbtion of Bispham-with-Norbreck Urban District in April 1918 'the Borough' stretched north to within a few yards of the centre of Cleveleys.

The cliffs to the north of the Gynn were popular with holidaymakers and, in all but name were 'Blackpool'. They were also eroding rapidly; the old Uncle Tom's Cabin had disappeared over the edge in 1907 and it was only a matter of time before the tramroad followed it. In truth, the tramroad itself had to take a little of the blame. For half its life it had been involved in litigation, in part to prove itself a railway rather than a tramway, thus cutting its rates contribution to the local authorities by 75 per cent. Bispham, deprived of a substantial rates-income from the tramroad, simply could not afford to carry out sea-defence works to save the cliffs and had to agree to a take-over by Blackpool.

Negotiations between the Tramroad Company and Blackpool Corporation were proceeding, albeit slowly, when a rumour spread that the Lancashire & Yorkshire Railway was interested in buying the line. The Mayor of Blackpool, Alderman Lindsay Parkinson swung into action. Personally, and without any brief from the Council he negotiated the purchase of the tramroad, then approached his fellow Councillors and offered to sell it to the Corporation for what he had paid for it!

It is still a matter for argument as to whether the rumour of purchase by the railway was genuine or put about by Parkinson himself in order to achieve his objective—the absorbtion of the tramroad into the Blackpool system. Not for nothing was the redoubtable Parkinson described by the *Blackpool Times* as 'a superman, double-endowed with foresight, accustomed to swiftness of decision, and lightning-like rapidity of action'.

Parkinson, like Cocker, Bickerstaffe of the Tower and Holland of the Winter Gardens before him, his contemporaries Sykes, Lumb and Cameron, Manager of the Tramroad, and like Thompson of the Pleasure Beach after him, was a man who made Blackpool and was made by it. Today, Parkinson's actions over the tramroad would bring banner headlines screaming impropriety and downright chickanery (and undoubtedly he would find himself in the hottest possible seat on television). In that gentler world of 1918 the Council, reassured by his confidence in the purchase took the hint and took the tramroad off his hands. He had, after all, suggested that if they did not 'another company' might be interested. Of course that other unnamed company *could* have been the dreaded Lancashire and Yorkshire Railway.

Blackpool Corporation took over the running of the Fleetwood line on 1 January 1920 and soon afterwards joined the Promenade tracks to the tramroad at the Gynn; it was now possible to run a tram all the way from South Shore to Bold Street, Fleetwood, and Blackpool's influence could be felt all the way. It was even suggested that Blackpool might soon take over the St Annes and Lytham trams, spreading the influence all round the coast from the Ribble to the Wyre.

Others were asserting their influence too. Under the Improvement Act of 1917, Blackpool had been empowered to build a new promenade south from South Shore to the Borough boundary at Squires Gate *and a tramway along it*. The trams coming down from the north carried the destination 'Pleasure Beach', a valuable piece of advertising for the company of that name. Once the tramway extension was complete would the trams still carry the same destination? The Pleasure Beach Company were determined they would, if at all possible.

By an Agreement dated 23 February 1917 between the Blackpool Pleasure Beach Company and the Corporation it was agreed that firstly, any land acquired by the Council south of the existing Pleasure Beach should not be used as a funfair but secondly, and importantly:

> A Destination Indicator bearing the words 'Pleasure Beach' shall be exhibited on the outside of all tramcars completing their southerly journey at South Shore for a period of 15 years from the date when the trams shall commence to run on the new promenade.

At that time, of course, the Fleetwood line was independent and the tramcars ran along the 'back' road to terminate at North Station, but with amalgamation it was possible, and desirable, to run them along the promenade as well down to the terminus at the Pleasure Beach. The Tramroad Company had never had to bother much about destinations and contented itself with route *letters*: 'F' meant Fleetwood, 'B' meant Blackpool; even 'P' could be taken for Promenade. But an agreement is an agreement, so the Fleetwood cars hung a metal plate on the front of the cars bound for 'Pleasure Beach'. However rudimentary, the advertising was carried, and the influence stretched all the way from the Velvet Coaster and the Virginia Reel to the Pharos Lighthouse and the Knott End Ferry.

In effect the agreement was more than honoured. When the

trams started running past the Pleasure Beach and along the new extension to the south they carried the destination 'New South Promenade via Pleasure Beach', and continued to do so for many years after the fifteen-year agreement expired in 1941. The present indication 'Starr Gate' is a comparatively recent innovation.

With amalgamation and extension came the last elaborations of the tramway system. At Fleetwood the line was taken in a loop to bring it alongside the ferry terminal; at the other end of the old tramroad line the track was joined to the track along Talbot Road to allow trams there to run along Dickson Road from the Gynn, round by Talbot Square and back to the Gynn by way of the Promenade. Both loops were in anticipation of running tramcars with trailers. At the southern end of the system the terminal loop for the new promenade extension was within a few yards of the St Annes line so a link was put in there. This made it possible to run a long-distance 'Circular Tour' all the way from Talbot Square by way of leafy Marton to Lytham Road, Squires Gate, round on to the Promenade and back to Talbot Square.

There was no finer way to spend a leisurely sunny summer afternoon than perched on the seat of an open single-decker 'toastrack' tram drifting gently round the tree-lined curves of Whitegate Drive, past the gates to the new Stanley Park, on to 'the Oxford' where the tram would pause (strictly against regulations) long enough for a street-photographer to snap the group (prints available 24 hours later). Then on the tram would go, round by Squires Gate, glimpsing the smart blue and white Lytham St Annes trams in their depot, perhaps to wave and call to a circular party making its way in the opposite direction, round to the sea-front again for a sprint up the Promenade to Talbot Square. Even if the journey were possible today it would be a nightmare of traffic lights, traffic jams and traffic fumes.

By the 1920s towns were beginning to abandon their trams and take to the buses; Blackpool itself ran buses but remained loyal to the tram as a means of moving the vast crowds thronging the resort. It was logical; a bus of the day carried some fifty passengers but a Dreadnought could swallow up eighty-six. It ran on its own right of way whereas the bus growled along in the increasing traffic. Until

1923 Blackpool bought its trams from various manufacturers but in that year started producing its own at the car sheds in Rigby Road.

Tramway enthusiasts have their own particular favourite design. For some it is the Manchester 'Pilcher' (named after the designer but naturally nicknamed 'Pilchards') or the Manchester 'California', which was very much like the San Francisco cablecar design. But by any standards the Blackpool designs of the 1920s are 'classics'. The double-deckers were capacious, some with open balconies, some closed. The paintwork was immaculate, coat after coat of primer laboriously rubbed down, then a sealer coat, two undercoats and a topcoat. The panels were lined out, the elaborate coat of arms transferred and then three coats of varnish were applied.

The results were elegant, with a decided 'touch of class'. They had to be for they had rivals sweeping in from the south—from classy St Annes. These luxurious trams, labelled 'Pullmans', were acknowledged as the most comfortable trams in Britain; again, they had to be, for the car and motor coach were developing rapidly.

Soon there were new trams for the Fleetwood route; spacious and modern, they were not just long but also wide—8in wider than the standard cars. The Blackpool *Gazette and Herald* took the opportunity for a sideswipe at London's efforts and chortled:

> The Blackpool trams, and particularly the latest models, are as comfortable as any to be found in the country and Londoners would probably go wild with delight were their own trams so comfortably appointed as the latest blue cars of Lytham St Annes. No one who remembers the type of tramcar in use thirty years ago can say there has been no improvement in design.

And yet, within ten years the design would be swept away and something radically new put in its place. The bus-lobby would be increasingly vociferous, towns would scrap their trams and Blackpool would teeter on the brink of following the fashion. Then it would go the other way and not only retain its trams but revolutionise them—all in the name of that one word on its coat of arms, 'Progress'. In doing that it would find a design and a mode of transport that reflected the changing times and matched the town's personality in those times. And yet another name would bounce on to the Blackpool stage.

10 The Blackpool Trams III

The thirties. Streamliners—new creations in ivory and green

The concept which revolutionised Blackpool's public transport system in the 1930s began, strangely enough, in Sunderland and among the precipitous streets of West Yorkshire. Preston helped it on its way, and what could be called the 'Yorkshire Mafia' in Blackpool oiled the wheels.

By 1932, Blackpool's tramway fleet was, to say the least 'variegated'. The 'Dreadnoughts' and some of the old Tramroad Company cars were thirty years old, there were various adaptations and conversions of other elderly cars, and the design of the 'new' trams of the 1920s was beginning to look out of date. The open 'toastracks' in particular looked archaic against the sleek motor-coaches pouring into the town. The Depression was biting, the holiday trade (and therefore the income from the trams) was stagnating, and the impact of the private car was beginning to be felt.

Fortunately, Blackpool's Transport Committee had the right Chairman, the indefatigable Alderman Thomas Lumb—yet another of the outstanding names tied irrevocably to the Golden Miles of the Fylde Coast. Lumb, together with Benjamin Sykes had conceived and executed the Blackpool to Fleetwood Tramroad and had masterminded the development along it.

Lumb was a particularly interesting character. By profession he was not only an engineer and surveyor but also an architect—at a time when the architectural world was being strongly influenced by the Garden City movement and the new architectural styles being demonstrated by Charles Rennie Mackintosh in Scotland, Edgar Wood in the North of England, Voysey, Walton and Mackmurdo nationally. All were influenced by the Secessionist movement on the continent.

In 1900, Lumb severed his connection with the firm of Garlick & Sykes and set up in practice as architect, surveyor and engineer. But he retained his interests, as consultant or director, in both the Cleveleys Hydro and the Norbreck Estate, and, importantly, he remained Manager of the Fleetwood Estate.

As an architect he designed the houses on the estate at Rossall Beach on Fleetwood Estate land. Although the houses there are known as 'the Dutch Village' they are far more representative of the contemporary style in vogue in England at the time. Symbolically, they line the road alongside the tramway, centered on the tramway stop 'Rossall Beach'.

Further houses followed, notably at Cleveleys Park (now known as Thornton Gate), where the famous Garden Estate Exhibition of 1906 was held. A house in West Drive bears this date. Across the road is a distinctively 'original' house (known, confusingly as 'the Dutch Cottage') demonstrating the principles not only of the exhibition but of the architectural and social preoccupations of the time.

Significantly, Lumb also had an involvement, dating from his 'Sykes' days with the English Electric tramcar works at Preston. Even more significantly, Lumb and Sykes were both Yorkshiremen as were so many of the Directors of the old Blackpool Tramway Company—as was Walter Luff, one of the applicants interviewed for the post of Manager when Charles Furness resigned the post in 1932.

In the event Luff came second to Charles Hopkins, Manager for the Sunderland Tramways. The decision may have been influenced by the fact that Sunderland were already carrying out a modernisation process (as Blackpool realised it must do) whereas Luff's employers, the West Riding Tramways Company had just abandoned their trams in favour of buses!

Then fate took a hand. Hopkins decided to stay in Sunderland, so the Committee went for the next name on the shortlist. Luff, and Lumb, therefore, the 'best interests' of the Estates and English Electric, came together in a powerful (and Yorkshire accented) combination.

By chance (but more likely by design) the ailing English Electric

Company, battered by the combined effects of the Depression and the closure of many town tramways, produced sketches for a revolutionary new tramcar at the precise moment that Luff and Lumb went to the market in search of one. It had all the right characteristics for Blackpool and none of the features necessary for anywhere else!

Luff took up his position on 1 January 1933 and if the anti-tram lobby imagined that his reorganisation and modernisation programme would involve scrapping the trams they were swiftly disillusioned. The designs for the new tram were presented to him, he inspected them, approved of them and asked English Electric to give him a firm price in time for the Committee Meeting on 20 February.

At that meeting Luff not only produced the design for the new tram for the Committee's approval but outlined a complete Five Year Plan for the modernisation of the tramways system, just six weeks after he took up the post. The question hangs in the air; was it Luff's plan, Lumb's plan (nurtured over many years perhaps) or the results of a brilliant partnership?

The Committee approved the reorganisation plan and accepted the new tram design. (Possibly it was impressed by the price-tag, which at £2,000, was no more than the single deckers for the Fleetwood route had cost five years before and no doubt a loss-leader to obtain the order.) Luff announced that the first of the new cars would appear on 21 June. English Electric would bring the design to production in four months!

A positive tidal wave of change hit the Transport Department, carrying all, including the Tramways Committee, before it. Luff changed the colour scheme of the trams from red and white to a smart green and cream. He presented a car in the new colours to the Committee at the March meeting and it approved. The same month after attempting to improve the loading entrances of one of the old Tramroad saloon cars, and failing, Luff scrapped it. Luff proposed improvements to the track to ease bottlenecks and increase the capacity of the system; here the pace would not be so frenetic—by the opening of the 1934 season would do!

Luff's tidal wave carried the Tramway Committee on from

approval to adulation. The first of the new trams arrived on 19 June in time to meet the deadline and in time to impress the delegates to the Annual Conference of the Municipal Tramways and Transport Association. By the time the proposal to buy further trams of this design came up in Council even the one-time anti-tram Alderman Tatham had been converted. More than that, he *admitted* he had. 'I have been a scrap-the-trams merchant for fifteen years', he admitted, 'and now I believe I have changed my mind. I have altered my mind because the man who is now the Transport Manager of Blackpool is working a revolution in the transport World.'

The prototype was a success and twenty-four more were ordered from English Electric, without inviting other firms to tender. Possibly aware of the close liaison between Luff, Lumb and English Electric some Council members attempted to have this matter debated. Lumb firmly squashed the attempt, *backed by Alderman Tatham* (proving, once again, that instant conversion so often produces the zealot). He even hinted at an infringement of patent rights should another firm try to produce a similar vehicle, 'There is not another firm making trams like ours', he said. 'They cannot. They are not allowed to. There are patent rights.' With all the dignity and authority invested in him as Mayor Alderman Tatham concluded, '*This is the way we progress in Blackpool.*'

The vehicle which impressed the erstwhile critic so emphatically and had caused so much activity in the 'Trolley wires of power' was innovative indeed; hardly any of the traditional tram features were incorporated, making its apparently rapid development all the more extraordinary. It had a centre entrance and a lowered floor to its 'vestibule' making access easy. It had comfortable upholstered seats, a coach-like interior finish, windows curving up over the roof and a sliding 'sunroof'. The driver had a separate cab, a seat (totally unique in the tramway world) and a windscreen wiper. The passengers had heaters and folding doors. The final touch of luxury was a clock.

And they were not trams; rejecting adjectives like 'luxury', 'de-luxe' (fashionable at the time) or 'Pullman', the new vehicles were christened 'railcoaches'. Stories concerning them (more than likely originating in the Press Office) abounded. There was the story of the elderly lady who was convinced she was on a No 5 bus. Gentlemen it was said removed their hats when entering, and a visitor from Manchester is supposed to have said 'When you step on it, you look around instinctively for a mat to wipe your feet on.' The *Gazette* joined in poetically:

> Some towns have trams of brown and blue
> And some of red and black.
> And some have trams of yellowish hue
> That send shivers down your back.
> Some paint their cars in stripes and stars
> But the finest I have seen
> Are Blackpool's new creations
> In ivory and green.

It was a triumph all round—for Luff, for Lumb, for English Electric, for Blackpool and for Progress.

These first railcoaches were certainly revolutionary and luxurious but they had a limited capacity—forty-eight seats (and no standing or smoking by order) compared with the eighty-six of the old Dreadnoughts. They were very suitable for the 'tramroad' run up to Fleetwood (they had, in fact exactly the same number of seats as the 'Pullmans' then running) but something more capacious would be needed for the busy Promenade routes in Blackpool.

An open-topped double-decker version of the railcoach was designed and a prototype presented for the approval of Blackpool's councillors. They were so impressed that they arranged a public exhibition. The *Gazette* joined in euphorically:

> The seats possess almost the comfort of a Chesterfield, complete with luxurious footwarmers. The driver is the luckiest in the world—a cosy compartment all to himself, plus a seat.

Then came Luff and English Electric's version of the popular 'Toastrack'. This was basically a railcoach without a top but with a neat canopy over the centre-entrance to take the trolley-pole rather than a stumpy mast, swept up panels at each end and a decided elegance to the whole design. Finally, in spite of Luff's predeliction for low-capacity cars a huge double-decker capable of absorbing ninety-four people at one gulp.

By 1935 a completely new fleet of trams was running in Blackpool which was no mean achievement in any circumstances, and considering the time and the question marks hanging over tramways in general a remarkable gesture of faith in future. Indeed, neighbouring Lytham St Annes decided to give up its trams in favour of buses in the same year. Also in that year Blackpool registered another 'first' when it decided to preserve one of the old Dreadnoughts. The *Gazette* had observed their passing after the 1934 season and commented:

> They were 'clumsy, awkward and dangerous' say the disciples of Progress. But they were Blackpool's own trams. And there was nothing like them anywhere else.

In March 1935 Luff announced that a Dreadnought would be preserved (the first electric tram to be honoured so). The *Gazette* delightedly observed:

> Sometime in the future, when there is a Pageant of Progress or something of the kind, it may be possible to resurrect the old car and parade it on the Promenade as a specimen of what people in Blackpool used to enjoy travelling on.

The Dreadnought does, as predicted by the *Gazette* so many years ago, parade up and down the Promenade at times, but some of the original 'Luff' fleet are still running in regular service, a tribute to the engineering craftsmanship of English Electric (and the later Brush of Loughborough Company) and the simple, robust nature of the concept (not to mention the constant care of the engineering workshops).

The one-man-operated (or rather, since Blackpool employs a fair percentage of women drivers, one-person-operated) cars which appeared in the 1970s look new—sleek, sharp-fronted and in the best traditions of the modern continental tramways—and are classified as new by the Department of the Environment. But lurking beneath the red and white colour scheme and hiding behind the deep masculine growl of its diesel-type hooter is a green and cream 1934 railcoach with a higher, feminine voice. The centre entrance became an exit, the front was extended to give a passenger entrance alongside the driver (and he was shifted from the traditional central 'tram' position).

The huge double-deckers are still running, modified only a little since they were introduced; *aficionados* can pick out an original covered top double decker from the open-tops which *became* covered in 1941. Even the 'Pride of the Fleet', the gleaming one-person-operated double decker which looks as new as any of the products running on diesel on the roads of every city in Britain is a rebuild of a 'balloon' double decker from the same batch of 1935 cars. Buses of 1955 are veteran items, carefully tended and brought out for shows; these trams are matter-of-fact everyday vehicles to people in Blackpool. They are a lasting tribute to the skill of the engineer and the advantages of simple electric traction (and, with ever-rising fuel costs must be an increasingly irritating thorn in the flesh to the bus manufacturers).

Blackpool went on to produce other new trams, including the ill-fated 'Coronation' of 1952. Too heavy and too expensive to run they did not survive. The English Electrics and Brushes of the thirties did, as did the open 'boat' cars. Dating from 1934 these are the oldest vehicles in the country still running in their original condition. They do not look a day over 1975 and they not only run in this country. Number 601 trundles round a museum track in Southern California. The sun may be brighter, the passengers more bronzed, but the turning circle looks remarkably like Little Bispham!

11 Pleasures and Palaces I

The Golden Mile and the Golden Triangle. Opera House, Winter Gardens and Grand Theatre

Blackpool's much publicised Golden Mile is barely a quarter of that length, with the Tower at one end and the Central Pier at the other. It gradually spread—south from the Tower end—taking over the gardens of the early Victorian villas of the old 'South Beach'. First the gardens were paved over and stalls erected, then more solid booths; the houses became open-fronted shops, cafés and so on.

Much of it was a turn-of-the-century development; what were houses in 1895 had, by the years of the promenade-widening of 1903–5, become part of the agglomeration, re-fronted and turned over to their new purposes. Even in the 1930s there were still isolated houses, guest houses and hotels within it. For all its image as a collection of tawdry peep and freak shows most of the Golden Mile was given over to *selling*—seafood, rock, souvenirs, buckets and spades and beach balls, 'jugs of tea for the sands', in fact anything that *would* sell!

Scattered along the parade were fortune tellers' booths (every 'Original Gipsy' there ever was it seems), cafés, amusement arcades and at least one larger covered funfair, Luna Park. But the highlights were the dubious sideshows, the despair of many a Watch Committee; fat ladies, two-headed (or was it five-legged) cows, freaks and fantastics of all descriptions.

It reached its peak (or depths) in the mid-1930s. The crowds of holidaymakers wanted some short sharp relief from the greyness of the Depression, and a showman by the name of Luke Gannon (which makes him sound like the black-hatted villain of a period 'Western') gave it to them. His approach was direct; present a sensation and advertise it 'big', using words the public would understand without any effort. 'Honeymoon Couple Starves For Love', screamed the billboard. 'Forty Days to Win £250. Divided in a Glass Case.' Every couple honeymooning in Blackpool (and there would be many) would understand what it meant.

When Gannon signed up the notorious Rector of Stiffkey, unfrocked for 'unmentionable' offences, he chose not merely to exhibit him but to show him 'starving' and in a barrel. The preoccupation with the lack of food was an essential attraction; the visitors were not exactly starving but money for food had to be carefully calculated and the essential four-meals-a-day tariff of the boarding house was part of the holiday blow-out. The barrel was a final indignity. The placard's approach was typical of the time 'Have *you* seen Poor Old Stiffkey? The Lad from the Village.'

The 1930s were hard and peculiarly ruthless. These were the days of marathon dance competitions, pole squatting (indignity again), Mosely, the Communists and the Jews battling it out in the East End of London, a spreading paralysis in the industrial areas of the North and a glittering 'Edge of Armageddon' scene in the West End (which seemed a million light-years away from the tarnished tinsel of the Golden Mile). Even the supposedly happy holiday-makers look grim-faced with women in dark practical clothes and men in ill-fitting jackets and trousers. The few men not wearing hats or caps look shaven-headed rather than short-back-and-sided. They would not look out of place in the Jarrow March, yet this was supposed to be Blackpool's heyday.

Stiffkey didn't starve to death, nor is there any evidence that the honeymoon couple did; in fact there is some evidence that every evening they clambered out of their glass coffins and tucked into fish and chip suppers like everyone else. Stiffkey went on across country to Skegness where he appeared in the company of a lion, which ate him.

Gone too is the Golden Mile, swallowed up by a gaudy, glittering series of huge slot palaces, a great bite taken out of its heart by a new access road. A goldmine it may be for its promoters, but the Golden Mile it is not.

Immediately behind the Promenade, bounded by the North Pier, the Winter Gardens and the Tower is the 'Golden Triangle' where Blackpool's heart beats strongly. The narrow side streets are jammed with pubs, cafés and a few grand restaurants, shops selling everything from high fashion through the shoddiest souvenirs and

A Grand Theatre programme cover, 1894

the tattiest trinkets to the inevitable Blackpool rock.

Here was its Victorian covered market, here is its new and controversial shopping centre. Here, on the Promenade, a few yards only from the Clifton (which began life as Mr Forshaw's Hotel) the change in lifestyles over the past thirty years is expressed under the name 'Lancastria'. In one building (and presumably owned by one perceptive firm) are the Lancastria 'Traditional Fish and Chips— Self Service'. Next door, is the Lancastria Steakhouse, above it 'the Old Lancastrian' 'A la Carte French Cuisine in Warm Jacobean Setting'. Times change, Blackpool changes, and along with it its entrepreneurs. Game, set and match to the Lancastria!

The octagonal ended building on the junction of Clifton Street and Talbot Road was Blackpool's first entertainment centre. It has housed at one time or another Assembly Rooms—the favourite coverall name for discreet Victorian pleasures—the Tivoli Cinema (née Theatre Royal), shops, grillroom and one of the biggest and best of Yates' Wine Lodges. Here, though, the champagne corks pop like machine gun fire. It is sold by the glass and it is considered perfectly proper to order 'another round'. Shocking though it may be for the purists it has even offered champagne on draught.

At the apex of the Golden Triangle is the Winter Gardens, older than and in some ways considered as a rival to the Tower. The Winter Gardens itself would consider the rivalry the other way round. It catered for the 'select' visitor and eventually included the Opera House, opened in 1889, designed by the incomparable Frank Matcham and a fitting setting for Tettrazini, Melba and Kreisler.

The Gardens themselves were opened in 1878 by no less a personage than the Lord Mayor of London. The *Preston Pilot* recorded that he was accommodated at the Imperial Hotel, part of the exclusive Claremont Park development on the northern cliffs. On the following day, 11 July, a Grand Procession formed for the journey down to the Winter Gardens. Sixty-three English towns were represented in it. It was recorded that no lady lower in rank than Mayoress was part of the representation. At the head of the procession were three 'state' carriages, at the rear a body of shareholders and the whole included four bands, a Corps of Volunteers and Mounted Police. In celebration there was a concert

The 'Marble Church' (1912) at Fairhaven, Lytham St Annes

The decorative pebble work in the sea-front gardens at Lytham St Annes

The 'Dutch Cottage' in West Drive, Cleveleys. It formed part of the famous Garden Estate Exhibition of 1906

The Ferris Wheel in Morecambe's Pleasure Park. Its diameter is 150ft

Blackpool's North Promenade. The colonnade is part of the 1924 works. In the distance are the cliff lift and boating pool

in the Winter Gardens Grand Pavilion and fireworks in the evening on both the North and South (now Central) Piers.

Then, in 1887 the legendary 'Bill' Holland took over the management. He expanded and elaborated the complex of buildings at the Winter Gardens. The Empress Ballroom, a rival to the Ballroom at the Tower, was his idea, but Holland died before it was completed. That year, too, the Great Wheel was erected. It towered over the Winter Gardens for thirty years and it and the nearby Tower became twin landmarks. It was 220ft in diameter, weighed 1,000 tonnes, its axle alone weighing 36 tonnes; there were thirty carriages, each holding thirty people and in two hours on its opening day 4,000 people took the exciting aerial ride. Again, it was not a total success and was finally demolished in 1928, a few months after the Winter Gardens Company had amalgamated with the Blackpool Tower Company.

But the most famous story attached to Bill Holland is an essentially personal, and intensely 'Blackpool' one. He ordered a 100-guinea carpet for his Winter Gardens—an expensive luxury but in line with his policy of giving the best to his patrons. His friends were critical: 'A 50 guineas carpet?', they said, 'for trippers to spit on?' Bill Holland saw the advertising value immediately. A billboard invited: 'Come to the Winter Gardens and Spit on Bill Holland's 100 Guinea Carpet.' Thousands came—and no one spat. Or, if they did, it was not recorded!

The expansion continued after Holland's death with new pavilions evoking the atmosphere of Spain or a baronial hall, a covered funfair and finally, in 1939, a replacement for the old Opera House.

Thomas Sergenson, a contemporary of Bill Holland and in some way a rival, had come to Blackpool in 1876 in connection with the Prince of Wales Baths and Theatre then being built on a site next to the Blackpool Aquarium and Menagerie. Holidaymakers were beginning to tire of the simple pleasures of the seaside and were hungry for entertainment. Between them, the Aquarium and Menagerie, Prince of Wales, Talbot Square Rooms and Winter Gardens were able to offer theatres, concerts, aquatic displays, 'spectacles' such as a representation of a fairyland grotto, halls depicting the Ruby Mines of Burma, and 'Gardens'.

The Prince of Wales was also used for evening classes in the winter, but the piers, in the early days, were for walking only (indulging the Victorian feeling that they *could*, with only a little help, Walk on the Water), and for boarding the many steamers offering pleasure trips up and down the coast, over to the Isle of Man or to far-away places like Barrow, Liverpool and Llandudno.

Sergenson took a lease on the new Prince of Wales building and soon had control of the Theatre Royal in Talbot Square, adding them to a quiverful of controlling interests in theatres across the North of England. But he wanted a theatre of his own, in Blackpool, naturally. In October 1887 he bought a site in Church Street and announced his intention of building a theatre there. At about the same time the Winter Gardens announced their intention of building a theatre, and mindful of the new manager's (Bill Holland) capabilities Sergenson suspended building plans in order to see what went on up the street at the Winter Gardens. Ironically, Sergenson and the Winter Gardens had commissioned the same architect, Frank Matcham.

However, Sergenson did not let his site lie idle. He built a number of shops and a large wooden building which opened as Ohmy's Circus in 1889. The same year the Opera House opened and was an immediate success. By 1891, with the foundation stone for the Tower complex laid (on the site of the Menagerie and Aquarium), it was time for Sergenson to reappraise his plans for the theatre. He commissioned as architect Frank Matcham, who had designed the Opera House; it was a wise (and ironic) move. There was to be one overriding consideration. Sergenson wanted, he said, 'the best, prettiest and cosiest theatre possible'.

At thirty-seven, Matcham was just one step from the top. He had been born at Newton Abbot, Devon, and apprenticed to a local architect and surveyor for whom he worked until 1875. In that year he moved to London and the practice of T. Robinson. In 1878 he married the boss's daughter and, when his father-in-law died a few months later, took over the running of the practice.

By 1888 he was designing theatres all over the country: the Alhambra in Brighton; the Mile End Empire; the Grand in

Islington; the Theatre Royal in Bury, and another Theatre Royal in St Helens—both in Lancashire; and the remodelling of the Grand in Douglas, on the Isle of Man. Between then and the time Sergenson approached him he was responsible for theatres in Ashton-under-Lyne, Southport, Great Yarmouth, Portsmouth and Liverpool; he had also established links with Sir Edward Moss and Oswald Stoll which were to be of great importance in the future.

The Grand Theatre opened in 1894, just a few months after the completion of the Tower, and by that time Matcham was engaged on theatres in Belfast, Birmingham, Wakefield, Brixton and Bolton. In 1900 he designed the 4,000 seat London Hippodrome (Talk of the Town) for Moss. It opened as a 'theatre-circus' and its supreme novelty was its water-tank, round which productions were created; 'spectaculars' like the 'Sands o'Dee' or 'the Typhoon' were staged there. Then, in 1904, he designed the London Coliseum for Oswald Stoll.

The Coliseum marked the change from music hall to variety; the individual artists were less important and more sophisticated 'scena' and sketches came to the fore. The new theatre offered four separate performances a day—the first at noon, the last at 9pm, and two separate programmes. An early programme shows that at the first and third performances one could see a 'musical scena' called 'The Pickle Girl', the setting described as 'Among the pickle jars of Brosse and Clackwell's', Bonita and her Cuban and African Midgets in an item entitled 'Coon Songs and Dance' and the performance concluded with a 'grand musical spectacle' 'Port Arthur' (this was during the Russo-Japanese War). The second and fourth performances featured 'Military evolutions' by the Lady Troupe of Japanese Guards, the Inimitable Society Entertainers Bella and Bijou, Madame Alice Esty presenting the mad scene from *Lucia di Lammermoor* (sic) and a 'grand musical spectacle' 'The Derby'.

The spelling of the Coliseum was queried by an academic of Oswald Stoll's acquaintance. 'I see', said the academic, 'that you have knocked the O.S. out of 'Colosseum'.' The supremely confident Sir Oswald replied: 'Yes. The O.S. out and the 'I' in!.'

The initials O.S. were virtually synonymous with the New Variety presentations of the time; the story was remembered for two generations.

After the Coliseum came the Palladium, then the Victoria Palace and in all Matcham designed over 200 theatres. In each, the Matcham personality is very apparent, yet he was not simply a decorator; great attention was paid to ventilation and heating, and he developed the use of structural steelwork in the inherent design of the building. Balconies were now cantilevered, not supported by pillars, sight-lines were carefully calculated and it was said that Matcham could make a 3,000 seat auditorium feel as initmate as one for 300.

Sergenson had asked for 'the prettiest' which was what he got; the Blackpool *Gazette*, in its report of the opening, called it simply 'Matcham's masterpiece':

> The great width of the theatre finds room for the most spacious pit, and upon the parquetted floor there must be sitting room for at least a thousand persons. The dress circle is sure to be a most popular part of the house. The upholstered tip-up seats provide for about a hundred and sixty, and behind there is a spacious saloon, charmingly decorated, together with a promenade which will provide standing room for many more. The upper circle will easily seat from four to five hundred, and here again the upholstery is in accord with the other parts of the house. The gallery will provide accommodation for at least one thousand, the view of the stage from every part being uninterrupted, so that not far short of three thousand persons may witness the performance at one time, all seated. There are handsome crushrooms, foyers and saloons, all parts of the house having separate retiring rooms, comfortably furnished and fitted with every convenience.

Striving for excellence, but aware of a background of improvisation and cheap-jack conversion (after all, Sergenson had been locked in battle with the authorities over the infringements of fire regulations at Ohmy's Circus), the *Gazette* turned its attention from the arrangements to the construction of the theatre, then to its decoration:

> The sanitary arrangements and ventilation are up to date in every particular, and special attention has been paid to the heating apparatus, by which the whole building can be warmed to any extent in winter.

Hydrants and fittings for protection from fire are placed in convenient positions whilst the electric light has been installed throughout [Gas lighting, elaborate draperies and imperfect fire escape routes resulted in something like 100 serious theatre fires in the years 1870–1900]. The fact that there are no columns to obstruct the view in any part of the house is a splendid feature of the building, and is accounted for by the fact that the framework, which is entirely of steel and of immense strength, is on the cantilever principle.

Encircling the proscenium arch are twelve small floral panels representing the months of the year. The background is cream, but gold is lavishly used, and blue—which is the prevailing colour throughout the theatre—is introduced to charming effect. At either side there are two magnificently-painted panels which do the artist every credit [presumably a staff artist employed by the Art Decorations contractors, Binns and Sons of Halifax].

The ceiling is also divided into panels radiating from a fine centrepiece from which hang the magnificent brass electroliers and upon these panels are inscribed in letters of gold the names of famous composers, including Sullivan, Lecocq, Collier, Soloman, Hervey, Offenbach etc. (an echo, perhaps, of the Tower Ballroom with its similarly inscribed panels) . . . Cream and Gold are also predominant colours in the beautiful plasterwork encircling the fronts of the upper tiers, while these are also relieved by prettily painted panels . . . and the Grand deserves to rank as one of the handsomest theatres in the provinces, and we do not doubt that both residents and visitors will make haste to speedily see it for themselves.

The theatre was to be 'grand' in every sense of the word. The opening production set the atmosphere—Wilson Barrett in *Hamlet*. Again, the local newspaper took the point:

Many managers have found that Shakespeare spells ruin . . . We take it as an earnest of the manner in which Mr Sergenson intends to conduct his new venture that he should elect to produce 'Hamlet' . . . on the opening night.

The reporter dutifully recorded the personalities present:

Evening Dress was general in the stalls, circle and boxes, and the scene presented at the rising of the curtain was a very brilliant one indeed. The stage boxes were taken . . . by Lady Queensbury and Mr and Mrs J. Nickson while the other boxes were engaged by Mr W. Holland, Mr Charles Iddeson (who thus gave a 'friendly lead' to a fellow manager) Mr G. L. Seed, Mr Matcham (the architect), Mr Wallworth (one of the contractors) while Mr Wilson Barrett also reserved one of the boxes for a party of ladies. Members of the Town Council were plentiful, among them being included Alderman John Bickerstaffe, Councillors Mather, Nickson and T. Bickerstaffe.

Strangely, the report does not mention that Alderman John Bickerstaffe was also the Chairman of the Blackpool Tower Company and could also be said to be giving 'a friendly lead' to Sergenson. Perhaps, as Chairman, he was not so directly associated as the fellow managers. The report observes:

> The ladies mustered a strong force and many charming first night costumes were in evidence in the stalls and circle. Altogether, the new Grand Theatre and Opera House received a good 'send off', for the audience was most enthusiastic throughout . . . The silk programmes in honour of the first night were exquisitely perfumed with the new 'Tower Bouquet' a charming scent which Mr H. Kettlewell of Church Street, Blackpool has just introduced.

It was, altogether, a glittering occasion, befitting a bustling, town of progress and maturity. It was also a far cry from the time; fifty years before a visitor had written despairingly: 'We hope you and Papa continue to improve and are in sufficient health to enjoy the amusements Buxton affords, you are very fortunate in possessing a theatre, I wish we had one here, if it were a pretty good one, for there are so few amusements.'

In his speech (given after three curtain calls) Wilson Barrett recalled his own experiences in earlier, less enlightened days:

> I am not very old, but still I can remember the time when Blackpool had but one little theatre, and, speaking from experience, the salaries were not great at that little theatre by any means. [Laughter, the newspaper reports!] Had it not been, I am afraid to say, for the liberality of some of the little landladies at the not-then-very-prosperous watering place, most of the actors would have had very small tables, and very little to put upon them to help them towards their arduous duties at night. I speak as one who knew and felt—and did not eat too much. [More laughter] But now I see you have your Tower, your theatres, gardens, palaces, and I say with all my heart 'Long may it improve as rapidly as it has done in the past.'

The Grand Theatre was off to a flying start and was always the 'prestige' theatre of the town. Briefly, in the thirties, it flirted with the talkies and annuallly provided a summer venue for a sure-fire comedy play, latterly featuring faces familiar on television. But the greatest drama featured not actors, but the Grand Theatre itself; the battle staged was, perhaps, less spectacular than 'The Derby' or 'Port Arthur' but the histrionics would have had the approval, surely of Wilson Barrett and the ghost of Frank Matcham, mourning the loss of so many of his exquisite theatres must have smiled a satisfied smile. But that was eighty years into the future and Blackpool had long to improve as rapidly as it had done.

12 Pleasures and Palaces II

The Tower and Progress. Raikes Hall and retreat. Echoes of well-remembered names

The Blackpool Aquarium and Menagerie opened in 1874 on the site previously occupied by Sir Benjamin Heywood's house 'West Hey'. In 1880 it was acquired, along with the adjoining Beach Hotel, by 'the Blackpool Central Property Company' headed by Dr W. H. Cocker, Blackpool's first Mayor. (He had, in fact been Mayor up to 1879). In 1889 this property, together with the New Market, was acquired by a London syndicate called the Standard Debenture Corporation Ltd whose aim was to duplicate the Eiffel Tower on some prestigious site in Britain—meaning, one presumes, Blackpool.

Blackpool's reaction was cool to say the least but the syndicate persisted, approaching the current Mayor, Alderman John Bickerstaffe and in February 1891 the Blackpool Tower Company was registered, with John Bickerstaffe as Chairman. His manoeuvering had convinced the local worthies that the Tower, albeit a proposal from 'outsiders' (and Londoners at that!) could benefit the town. So, less than twenty years after it had been opened, the Aquarium and Menagerie was demolished, its facilities to be included in the new Tower complex.

The foundation stone was laid on 29 September 1891 and the building was officially opened on Whit Monday, 1894. It rained— and the crowds flocked in to see the splendid new building and to crane their necks upwards, into the rain, to gaze at the 518ft structure towering above the ornate terra-cotta facade.

Behind the facade was, as promised, a menagerie (later the home of the legendary 'Wallace' whom Albert Ramsbottom assaulted with his stick with an 'orse's 'ed 'andle and got 'et), aquarium and a series of galleries, conservatories, bars and cafés. A circus seating 3,000 spectators was housed *between* the legs of the Tower in the centre of the building and on the north side was the Tower Ballroom, probably the finest Victorian Baroque interior in the country. The huge parquet dance floor was circled by two balconies divided into intimate sections, for all the world like theatre boxes, ceilings were elegantly painted, everything hung with ornate plasterwork, gilded, festooned, set off by intricate lamps and electroliers. It was the kind of architecture usually found only in the most luxurious palaces of Europe, and here it was the happy hunting ground of everyone. It was simply breathtaking. And it still is.

The circus was nothing new. Ohmy's circus was established up the road and travelling circuses were a feature of many towns. But the setting was vastly different to the flapping Big Top or the ramshackle structure on the site of the Grand. The legs of the Tower spread wide enough to enclose the whole auditorium; as spectacle was the order of the day the whole ring could be flooded to provide a 'water ballet' finale or, when the times were warlike, to stage a model sea-battle.

And rising above the 5 million bricks of the building itself was this exciting single finger pointing to the sky (and virtually shouting the motto of the town 'Progress'). The Tower Ascent was itself a commodious hall and the journey up exciting. From the top of the Tower the Victorian crowds had a bird's eye view down on to the town, back over the rolling Fylde to the Pennines beyond.

For a short time the Tower had two sisters—up the coast at Morecambe and down at New Brighton, but they didn't last. The Blackpool Tower was triumphant. It attracted the spectator to its menagerie, aquarium and ballroom balconies, the intrepid to its tower-top. It attracted the dancers, the audiences to its circus and children's ballets in the ballroom. In the wet weather it attracted, it seemed, everybody! It built up its own stars—the clowns Doodles and Coco, Reginald Dixon, Ena Baga and the 'Wonder Wurlitzer'—all equally famous, and, of course 'Wallace' (who never existed, though every child visiting the menagerie knew he was there).

The Tower gave the town a trademark (there's a Tower Cab Company) and an instantly recognisable symbol. Use the symbol and there is no need to mention the name of the town. It was as effective and unique an advertising gimmick as the 'Scchh' of Schweppes. It marked (and marks) journey's end for the approaching holidaymaker, visible miles away across the fields; every electricity pylon on the Fylde side of Leyland has been mistaken for it by some eager child.

For all its prominence, the Tower does not dominate; it beckons and welcomes. During the Illuminations it becomes a setpiece in itself, with lights zipping up and down it (and, at times, a searchlight sweeping the sea from the top). In summer it is decorated with flags—not one at the top to mark the pinnacle but strings apparently holding it down to the four corners of the building. They must be the biggest strings of the biggest flags in the world!

The Prince of Wales Baths and Theatre alongside, built in 1877, survived until 1899 when it was demolished and the Alhambra erected on its site. Here was another splendid building, a sumptuous theatre, a second circus and its own ballroom. The theatre again big, was a 3,000 seater, the circus only a little smaller than the Tower one next door; but times were changing. It went into receivership in 1902, but reopened as the Palace two years later. This time it succeeded. Blackpool was expanding again, times changed for the better and the Palace combined variety and talkies. Then, with times changing again, it was demolished in the 1960s and along with it went the County, one of Blackpool's oldest hotels and in its place rose a huge department store.

In the shadow of the Tower stood (one is tempted to say *crouched*) other, less ostentatious, but no less important, entertainment centres. There was Feldman's Theatre—symbolically just off the Promenade but facing it—at Hound's Hill and theatres and pavilions were built on the developing North and Central Piers. The theatre on the North Pier, indeed, became one of Blackpool's premier ones, for years the venue for Lawrence Wright's *On With The Show* and later the home of the beloved Northern comedian, the near-blind Dave Morris.

Morris was in the tradition of the North of England comedians—Frank Randle, Norman Evans, Jimmy James, Albert

Modley—in that he established an instant and personal friendship with each member of the audience; the same could not be said of, for instance, Formby, and even less of Max Miller. His catchphrase summed it up: 'If you ever come to Blackpool, look me up.' There is a story told of a famous occasion when he was doing a radio broadcast with a totally blind pianist as a supporting act. The lights in the studio failed and Morris immediately ad-libbed, 'Come on, lad, we can carry on if nobody else can!'

Frank Randle's name will forever be linked with Blackpool (which he eventually made his home). His humour was instantly recognisable: the complications of, for example, sewing on a button, the eccentric, toothless aged hiker, the 'callsign' of a resounding belch. It was a kind of vulgarity that, in effect, gave no offence because it *was* instantly recognisable as the natural thing for that eccentric character. He would explain—in the inevitable story about visiting a pub—'I had to go to th' lav. I put a note next to mi glass saying "I have spit in this ale!" When I got back somebody had written underneath "So have I!" But I drank it.' Then, 'I said to th' landlord "By 'eck! This ale's thin!" He said, "Tha'd be thin if tha'd come up th' same pipe as that!" ' In retrospect, it all seems curiously innocuous, vulgarity taken to the point where it becomes almost attractive.

Randle matured to films, notably the ramshackle (but highly successful) films produced by Mancunian Films in a tiny converted chapel in Rusholme. One, *It's a Great Life*, made in 1952, preserves most of Randle's 'business' for posterity and, if nothing else, is a tribute to his sheer versatility. The setting, in those days of National Service was an army camp, with Randle wreaking havoc, if not as a rogue elephant at least as a rogue rabbit. The film was made on a shoestring (a local schoolyard used as the parade ground, a 'battalion' of extras drawn from the University Training Corps, and supplying their own uniforms!), Randle's supporting stooges from his stage show and the very young Diana Dors desperately trying to keep up with the gangling ad-libbing Randle. Everything was built round Randle, or rather his many acts. It is an extremely long film!

Stories about Randle are legion and often exaggerated. He had, to put it delicately, a drink problem and was once taken into custody after a slight accident with a tram on Blackpool Promenade. The magistrate admonished him, but Randle was defiant. 'It was the tram's fault', he insisted. 'It came straight at me!' 'Well,' said the magistrate, 'you were driving on the tram-reservation.'

Men like Randle *were* Blackpool in the thirties, forties and fifties. Their open and honest vulgarity was harmless. There was no mawkishness, no sugary sentimentality ('Mother' inevitably meant 'in-law', not a figure to be sweetly sung about). Like the town, they gave value for money, at whatever cost to themselves.

The 'superior' North Pier had its own orchestra, under the baton of one 'Toni'; again the name is synonymous with the town. 'Toni and the North Pier Orchestra' needed no additional 'Blackpool'. His tradition was that of the Palm Court and generations of holidaymakers relaxed in deck chairs in the relative comfort of the glassed-in enclosure imagining the Irish Sea to be the blue Mediterranean of Monte Carlo.

The entertainment centres of the Golden Triangle could absorb thousands of visitors on a rainy day and drew them, like a magnet to that strip of promenade and the narrow streets behind, less than 60,000sq m in all. Inevitably, there were casualties. Before the days of the Tower holidaymakers could be attracted inland to the delights of the Royal Palace Gardens at Raikes Hall. In essence, it was the same concept as the Winter Gardens but far bigger, more imaginative and capable of being a great success.

The estate surrounding the old Raikes Hall was turned into a mini-resort in 1871, before the days of the Winter Gardens, Prince of Wales, or Aquarium and Menagerie. There were pleasant groves, shady paths, gardens, a large conservatory and *seventeen bars*. A boating lake was formed and a track built for the popular sport of trotting. There was a monkey house, an aviary and a 'dancing platform'.

The indications were that the Royal Palace Gardens could become a major attraction; the nearest equivalent would be Belle Vue in Manchester, a variety of entertainment and amusement within a special 'park'; indeed, in 1888 the proprietors of Raikes Hall Gardens bought the old Golden Jubilee Exhibition building from Manchester and re-erected it over the old open dancing stage. They also erected a ballroom, using an old circus building to do it.

A special attraction intended for the gardens was a huge panoramic picture 'Niagara' painted by the French artist Phillipoteaux which would need a purpose built building to house it. Unfortunately, with the building half-finished the money ran out, the concessionaire superintending the project also ran out, and the proprietors were forced to finish the building. The spectacle was unveiled—admission 6d, but the crowds never came. On the opening day only seven people arrived—the next day nine. The admission price was reduced to 3d, but 'Niagara' was a flop.

The outdoor attractions were, on the whole, more popular, with acrobatic displays, even agricultural shows. The variety theatre was definitely popular; Marie Lloyd did not appear at the Gardens as many believe, but Gus Elen did, as did Katie Lawrence (less well remembered than the song she made famous 'On a bicycle built for two').

Later, with the shadow of the Tower looming over the gardens in more ways than one, there was a brief Indian summer—or, rather, African. 100 Zulus and Matabele and white South Africans, both Boer and English staged a spectacular show *Savage South Africa*. But throughout its history, Raikes Hall seems to have been dogged by the most unfortunate disasters. The owner of 'Niagara' ran out, storms damaged the conservatories and blew down the firework stands. The Boer War, and some not inconsiderable street battles, put an end to *Savage South Africa*.

The Royal Palace Gardens had their memories. Memories of Blondin, then in his seventies, doing his daring tight-rope walking act. But even there, the Fates stepped in; carrying his middle-aged son on a pole as a finale to his act, Blondin strained his back and had to terminate his season prematurely. For Blondin, if not for the management, the accident had its compensations; nursed back to health by a chambermaid at the Station Hotel he proposed marriage and was accepted.

Shortage of cash, rather than shortage of ideas or talent seems to have been the root-problem all along. The gardens had an excellent manager for many years in Charles Iddeson (who was in a box in company with Bill Holland of the rival Winter Gardens on the opening night of the Grand), and the setting was superb. Even being inland had its advantages; the rising ground towards the sea sheltered the gardens from what could be a cutting west wind. But looking towards the crest of the hill Iddeson and the visitors to the gardens could see the Tower—and the shadow it cast.

The combination of Tower, Alhambra (Palace) and Winter Gardens was too much. They drew the crowds back to the Golden Triangle and away from Raikes Hall. It was half a mile—a gentle stroll away from the gleaming new tower, the slowly turning great wheel, the 'pavilion'd in splendour' delights of the Winter Gardens and Matcham's Masterpiece—but it might as well have been half a million miles. The crowds stayed within the Golden Triangle.

But the Royal Palace Gardens went out in something of a blaze of glory with every misfortune combining to produce the most spectacular flop Blackpool had ever witnessed. A fast-talking, fast-moving American showman announced that he was going to organise a World's Fair (no less) in the Gardens. A circus and a big variety show arrived, then sideshows, closely followed by a unique attraction 'Leonie Clark's Boxing Kangaroos'. All was hustle and bustle, contractors working flat out for the opening deadline.

It was June, and the holiday season not yet begun. No crowds appeared and the only queue was that made up of joiners, riggers and overall contractors waiting to be paid. But they couldn't be; the American entrepreneur was relying on the first week's takings to pay them. Reassuring tham as best he could, he went off to London 'to raise funds', and was never seen again.

The showpeople packed up and left, hoping for a summer season in some less salubrious resort under some more solvent management. The sub-contractors drifted off sadly, sensing the bailiffs knocking at the door. The riggers and joiners and bricklayers camped out on site. They threatened, indeed, to burn the place down. The final funeral pyre was averted by the police who moved in and cleared them off, but shortly afterwards the Royal Palace Gardens was sold off for building purposes. Perhaps a final gigantic blaze would have been a fitting ending. It would have made a splendid sight from the turning wheel or the top of the Tower!

13 The Blackpool & Fleetwood Tramroad

An ideal and a goldmine, then John Bull *growls*

Many books about the Lancashire Coast tend to pass off the sandy miles between Blackpool and Fleetwood in a brief couple of paragraphs, if that, in order to get down to the more familiar nitty-gritty of neatly-documented Fleetwood or the more easily manageable rural delights of Thornton. In *Holiday Lancashire* Sydney Moorhouse refers to the stabilising factor of the sea defence works and H. C. Collins, the doyen of Lancastrian (rather than 'Lancashire') writers professes open dislike and says he sees 'no beauty in this stretch of desecrated coastline and only come this way in order to visit Rossall'.

Yet both refer to the tramroad linking Blackpool to Bispham, Norbreck, Anchorsholme, Cleveleys, Rossall and Fleetwood. It was the building of the tramroad which provided the spur for the development along its line. Surely that fact is cause enough for investigation?

Just as convenient river crossing became the location for early settlements, and canals and railways prompted the development of many later towns, so the Blackpool & Fleetwoood Tramroad brought about the development of the settlements—and by design, not by accident.

By the mid-1890s Blackpool was a successful, bustling and sizeable town. Its promenade stretched from the newly-opened Victoria (South) Pier to Talbot Square and work was beginning to extend it further north towards the Borough boundary at the Gynn. It had had its trams for some ten years, property development had spread its villas over Fumblers Hill to the Gynn Inn and now it had its Opera House, Winter Gardens, Grand Theatre and its new Tower. Soon the trams would begin to run down to St Annes and Lytham and work would begin on a widening (or rather a second widening) of the central section of that famous Promenade.

Even so, Blackpool was pausing, drawing breath for the biggest expansion yet. There was money and there were enterprising men (and, most importantly enterprising men with money) and there were ideas in the air. The internal combustion engine might still be a toy but steam was giving way to electricity up and down the country. The first Zeppelins were flying and shortly the Wright Brothers would be winging their way over sandhills at Kitty Hawk not unlike those at Squires Gate. Down on the ground newly-rich people were building a new generation of gracious houses and newly-rich industrial towns were building opulent town halls.

First the Arts and Crafts movement, then the garden city ideal had caught the imagination of the turn-of-the-century man; already he was recognising the evils and degradation of the dark satanic mill towns and determining to replace them with something better. Once again, the particular combination of history, landscape and people was to come into play, this time moulding the wilderness of sandhills and low cliffs to the north of Victorian Blackpool.

And once again extraordinary men with ordinary everyday names were the prime movers. The names are almost the definitive Northern ones—Sykes and Lumb, forenames Benjamin and Thomas. Together they combined the talents of engineer, surveyor and architect and both had flair and expertise.

Benjamin Sykes was a local man who had established his reputation during the building of the first 'new' promenade between Talbot Square and South Shore in the 1860s. The idea, proposed by Sykes and Lumb for a rail link between Blackpool and Fleetwood was not original; Sykes had been involved with an earlier proposal for a steam tramway from Lytham all the way round the Fylde Coast to Fleetwood in 1877, which itself had been a re-working of a project to extend the railway which entered Blackpool from the south along the coast to Fleetwood.

In the USA, the electric interurbans were pushing out across country from the city centres and along their tracks were developing well-planned, spacious suburban estates. These were not railways in the traditional sense of the word, nor were they lumbering street-tramways trundling along through the traffic.

They ran on their own rights-of-way and had (frequent) halts rather than stops. One of them, in fact, linked the city centre of Los Angeles to a developing suburb named Hollywood; the long, bogied interurban electric car can often be glimpsed in the early location filming there. More than once the Keystone Cops narrowly missed being flattened by one and on one memorable occasion Laurel and Hardy, were squashed, together with a formidable Ford Model T between two!

Lumb saw the combination of electric interurban tramway and 'garden city' development as an ideal—and one he and Sykes could bring to fruition between Blackpool and Fleetwood. Their aims were not entirely altruisitic, for both had involvements with the companies owning much of the land along the proposed line.

Lumb was Managing Director of the Fleetwood Estate Company, which controlled the area from Fleetwood to Rossall. Sykes was the agent for the Thornton Estate, whose land stretched from Rossall to just south of Cleveleys. Next came the land surrounding Eryngo Lodge and here Sykes' involvement was even more solid. He owned it and planned to turn it into a 'hydropathic establishment'. To the south again were several small estate lands and then the estate which stretched along the cliffs from Norbreck to the Blackpool side of Bispham and which belonged to the Norbreck Estate Company—proprietor Benjamin Sykes. Finally, on the very edge of Blackpool Borough, was the Gynn Estate, where Lumb acted as advisor to the owning syndicate.

So, when Sykes and Lumb made their proposals for a tramroad link between Blackpool and Fleetwood they knew there would be little opposition from the local landowners! They could not be so sure about the reactions of the local authorities at either end of the line—Fleetwood and, particularly, Blackpool.

Fleetwood raised no opposition; indeed it was enthusiastic. Remote at the end of its peninsula, it had to rely on the railway for efficient communication and the tramway would provide an attractive alternative. Although not yet sixty years old, Fleetwood was already a flourishing town needing a local public transport system of a kind not provided by the railway.

Blackpool was a different matter; it had taken over the previously private-owned tramway system in 1892 and would clearly not take kindly to a rival system within part of the town. Blackpool had spread north to the Gynn and was already casting envious eyes on the wide-open clifftop acres over the boundary in Bispham—the very acres to be traversed by the tramroad.

But Blackpool had a problem. It wanted to extend its promenade round from Talbot Square to the Gynn, and that needed constructional materials. The Gynn Estate had ample supplies of fill material along the top of its cliffs. The solution to the problem was obvious. No doubt acting on the advice of its consultant, Thomas Lumb, the Estate Company agreed to supply Blackpool with its materials, in exchange for the rights to build a section of tramway within the borough. A neat, and typically practical, 'Blackpool' solution! In May 1896 Blackpool Corporation granted a twenty-one-year lease of the section of the line from North station (then Talbot Road) to the Borough boundary north of the Gynn and the Act was passed through Parliament unopposed.

The prospectus for the line was published in June 1897. Sykes had established a company to carry out constructional work and brought in another influential name—T. S. Turnbull, a Manchester-based solicitor to co-ordinate the financial arrangements. The results are typical of the time: a successful arrangement brought about quickly and efficiently through personal contact between men who knew and trusted each other. Construction began in July 1897 and was complete less than a year later. Such was the drive and efficiency of the men of the project.

The concept was not entirely novel. In the Isle of Man the electric tramway from Douglas to Groudle Glen and Laxey had been running for some five years. John Cameron, a man who was to exert a mighty influence on the Blackpool & Fleetwood line, came from the Isle of Man (where he had been General Manager of the Manx Northern Railway and consultant to the Douglas–Laxey tramway). He became the General Manager and Secretary of the Company. The design of the tramcars was virtually identical to that of the narrow-gauge Manx line.

The regular service over the line began in July 1898, but not, at first, over the whole line. The Board of Trade Inspector objected to

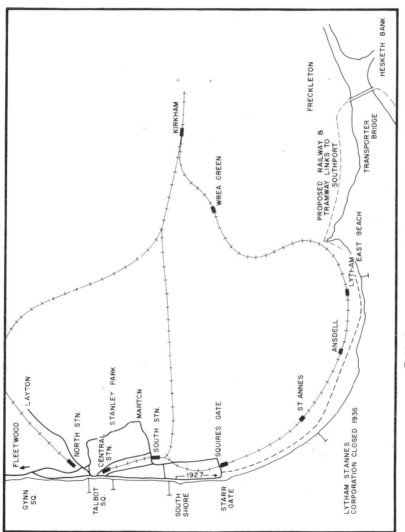

Fylde Coast tramways and railways c1930

the 'street' section of the line between the Gynn and Talbot Road station. The cars had been built 5in wider than originally specified and, as the road was narrow, the tracks had been laid close together. The trams simply could not pass each other. Blackpool was faced with a choice: either interlace the tracks (to eliminate the possibility of an accident by default) or widen the road. Blackpool chose the expansive alternative and widened the road to allow for adequate clearance. In the meantime, the service began from the Gynn.

The tramway was an immediate success. Well over 500,000 people used the line in the first six weeks, putting a considerable strain on the ten tramcars available and the rudimentary power supply. The through fare to Fleetwood was 6d ($2\frac{1}{2}$p) with intermediate 1d stages. Looking back over eighty-odd years the fare seems incredibly cheap; it is important to realise that the present day equivalent would be something around 70p in real terms—which is roughly what it is! However, the line made a handsome profit of £8,584 in the period from July to December 1898 out of a gross income of £12,476. Not surprisingly, the company immediately made plans to buy extra rolling stock and produced a first embryonic plan for an alternative line to Blackpool by way of Poulton-le-Fylde.

Travelling on the line in its early days must have been an exhilarating experience. An early advert extolls the attractions of the line in remarkably racy prose:

> For a fare of 6d each way you can enjoy an EIGHT MILE RIDE in luxurious Cars through unrivalled Coast and Country Scenery. A variety of magnificent views—across the Bay of Morecambe to Barrow and the Mountains beyond, and through a stretch of Beautiful Countryside teeming with old traditions and old associations.
>
> Visitors should go on the cars to Fleetwood and see the many sights—the extensive Docks and Shipping, and Fine Promenade.
>
> Cars leave the Gynn and Dickson Road every few minutes in the Summer and every quarter-hour in the Winter—when the cars are heated.

The journey began prosaically enough, in the shadow of Talbot Road railway station and well out of sight of the sea. The trams ran along a normal street-tramway as far as the Gynn where they swung not merely on to the sea-front but on to the very edge of the cliff with little between them and the beach below. It was a steep climb from the old Gynn Inn to Uncle Tom's Cabin, which disappeared over the cliff in 1907 to be replaced by a more respectable-looking building (in what was known as 'free Renaissance style') on the safer landward side of the road.

The cliffs were totally wild and apart from the newly-built sea-front road alongside the tramway there was nothing on the landward side either. This first climb brought the tramway to its highest point—virtually 100ft above sea-level. It was here, at the old Blackpool boundary that the tramroad 'proper' began—no longer a street tramway or one laid on a paved reservation at the side of the road but a roadside railway with sleepered track, lineside fencing and the central line of poles supporting the overhead wires reaching away into the distance.

The cars ran (contemporary accounts frequently used the word *skimmed*) along the open cliffs, the line occasionally easing its gradient by way of a cutting to Bispham where the Company had its depot a little way inland. Today, Bispham resolutely faces the sea, spreading along its own Queen's Promenade, but in those days Bispham meant the old village inland (and downhill from the breezy cliffs).

On the tramway went, to Norbreck, with its old Hall, now part of an expanding hydropathic establishment. Even as late as 1932 the coast road ended here, Anchorsholme lane swinging well inland behind the Hydro to reach Cleveleys by the back way. But not the tramroad; it skimmed on to Little Bispham where it left the cliffs to curve down through a sizeable cutting to Anchorsholme and Cleveleys. There was a scattering of farmsteads, thatched cottages and a few villas here where the line crossed Ramper road, (re-named Victoria road in honour of Her Majesty's diamond jubilee the year before). And from here the line ran almost level, just a little way away from (and barely above the level of) the sea. At Rossall, hard by the school, the line turned sharply to the east, as if to gather itself for the approach to Fleetwood.

Even today, this short section of the line still runs remote from the busy main road and one can still get a vague impression of what the original journey must have been like. Fleetwood is the only place in the UK where one can still travel on a street tramway. The last three quarters of a mile is a stately progress down the centre of the main road, cars and lorries taking second place, waiting patiently (or fairly patiently) behind until the tram takes on its load of holidaymakers and local shoppers.

Until 1925 the tramroad terminus was a straightforward one in the middle of Bold Street, but in that year the tramway was extended round the block to a loop alongside the Knott-End ferry slip and in the shadow of Decimus Burton's elegant Pharos. It is a remarkable juxtaposition—ferry boat battling with the fast-moving currents at the river-mouth, sleek modern railcar waiting on the loop with the classical lighthouse beyond.

Having established the tramroad, Sykes and Lumb turned their attention to the estate lands alongside. 'The best town planner', Lumb had said 'is a light railway or tramway'. He envisaged a series of well-planned, well-controlled settlements using the facility afforded by the line, and soon the sandy plain was dotted with neat villas and budding gardens. And soon, Cleveleys was known as 'the Garden Village'.

In 1906 it became the site for an exhibition of small houses, designed to encourage the garden village ideal and to demonstrate the wisdom of such ventures. The ideal was hardly new—one can trace its ancestry back to Ebenezer Howard, to Letchworth, to Titus Salts at Saltaire (and the supporters had an elegant middle-class example just round the corner in St Annes and a more workaday example just up the road in Fleetwood). Edgar Wood was building his evocative houses up and down the North of England and was gradually scaling down his mansions to establish the pattern of small, family-sized homes for three generations to come.

Similarly established was a *style* of living; a little more expansive and a lot more pleasurable than the style set earlier, in the manufacturing towns. After all, this was the seaside and this was the twentieth century.

Some of these early houses are immediately identifiable today— marked out by their attention to detail, their 'personal' style standing out against the mediocrity of later development. A clutch of semis at Thornton Gate and two terraces a little further north

The tramroad station at Cleveleys, 1981

along the main road are instantly recognisable; on the eastern side of the tramroad stands the 'Dutch Cottage' and its attendant houses around the West Drive development. Old photographs show the houses standing new and pristine in the open fields; now they are almost hidden by mature trees and flourishing gardens. In the best possible sense they are all the better for the foliage.

The developments—and the lifestyle—went on until Cleveleys linked up with Blackpool and almost with Fleetwood. There was the Grove Estate, Cleveleys Hydro Estate, West Drive, Shaw's Estate, Haddle House Estate, Crescent Estate and Anchorsholme Lane Estate, sweeping away the farms and cottages, lapping like the sea itself at the edge of Thornton village, then submerging it for ever. Whatever the intention, Cleveleys became a spreading, gentle town of modest homes, virtually an extension of northern Blackpool but resolutely unlike it. In the 1920s it was predicted that Cleveleys would soon be (as Bispham had already been) incorporated into the Blackpool Borough. It didn't happen; when reorganisation came Cleveleys became part of the Borough of Wyre—still resolutely 'apart' from its giant neighbour.

Blackpool became a giant in the early years of the twentieth century. The resorts of the Lancashire Coast were now easily accessible with the railways at the peak of their development. The Lancashire & Yorkshire, although a small railway by national standards, carried the bulk of the traffic to and from Southport and Blackpool; towns like Rochdale, Bury, and Bolton had their own services to the coast avoiding Manchester. Southport was linked to Liverpool by two competing lines and fast express trains— businessmen's 'Club' trains also—linked Southport and the Fylde Coast to Manchester. Travellers from east of the Pennines could reach the Fylde Coast by way of the link between Todmorden and Burnley or by way of the Rochdale–Bury–Bolton line which also gave access to Southport. The Lancashire & Yorkshire's main routes ran east–west, the way the holiday traffic wanted to go.

The London & North Western joined with the Lancashire & Yorkshire in running the line from Preston to Blackpool and Fleetwood and had its own branch from Lancaster to Morecambe; the Midland Railway brought the traffic to Morecambe Bay from Yorkshire. And from Fleetwood and Heysham the ships brought traffic from Ireland. Even Knott End on the eastern side of the Wyre had its own railway, trundling across the flat acres of the Fylde to Garstang; a 'brief' railway, this, completed in 1908 and closed in 1930.

Excursion traffic had increased to such an extent that both Blackpool North and Central Stations had to be rebuilt and enlarged. In 1898 work at Blackpool North was completed, giving the station general platforms with a total length of 3,600ft and excursion platforms 6,300ft. Three years later the new Central Station was completed and this had a total of 8,888ft of platform space. Tracks were duplicated and a completely new 'cut off' line (avoiding Lytham and St Annes) was built from Kirkham to Blackpool. Of no significance for normal traffic, this line, opened in 1903, was built simply for the excursion traffic of the summer. Such was the 'value' of Blackpool to the railways!

The North of England was at its peak—moneyed, confident to the point of arrogance. Blackpool reflected the North; it was 'pavilion'd in splendour and girded with praise'—far and away the

Thornton Mill, Cleveleys

most successful resort anywhere in the country, with all the trappings of success and not afraid to show them. The town was invited to exhibit at the Imperial Exhibition in 1909—and declined. The *Blackpool Times* commented gruffly:

> Evidently the management of the Imperial Exhibition does not welcome Blackpool's refusal to have anything to do with the Health and Pleasure Resorts section. Blackpool leads other health resorts and it is obvious that with Blackpool out of it the resorts of the United Kingdom cannot be fully represented.
>
> Nothing is so obvious to the people of Blackpool that what we want is that the holidaymakers of the United Kingdom should come to Blackpool and spend their days and weeks of rest here in the town itself and not go to a London exhibition.

Arrogant or confident, it was an undoubted fact that the exhibition would be the poorer with Blackpool out of it. And Blackpool knew it! It dazzled the visitors with its splendours, brainwashing them into suspending belief. A Belfast newspaper columnist recorded his first impression of the town:

The first sight of the Blackpool promenade is, without exaggerating, quite sufficient to take one's breath away with amazed admiration . . .
. . . the four mile macadamised road with its roadway, its three footpaths, double row of tram rails, the whole way along a most glorious stretch of hard yellow sand and magnificent wave-tossed sea . . . every tongue under the sun from broad Lancashire to Russian and from German to Spanish.

In 1891 the population was 24,000. By 1911 it was 58,000, a spectacular increase but still a town of manageable proportions. And 'managed' it was, by a hard core of businessmen who were as enterprising and as ruthless as their counterparts running the mills of Lancashire and Yorkshire. The idealism of the Cleveleys estates or the guiding hand of the building companies in St Annes was not for them. They wanted Bigger, Better, First, and the enthusiasm occasionally overbalanced into obsession. A plan to develop the Warbreck Hill estate (north of the Gynn and bordering on Bispham) as a garden suburb in the Cleveleys style was dropped in the last days of 1908. The *Blackpool Herald* commented sadly:

Another pretty ideal is driven to the wall by the passion of expanding. We looked for something of novelty and variety on the Warbreck Hill estate and it will now presumably pass into building hands, every inch to be covered with bricks and mortar.

The small voice of criticism was lost in the tumult of expansion and innovation. It was the hundreds of thousands of summer visitors who made Blackpool what it was, not a few hundred residents looking for homes by the sea. Then, a few weeks later a larger—and far louder voice condemned the whole place out of hand. On 1 May *John Bull* bellowed:

This popular resort is a place where the virtuous young woman or well-brought up youth would stand a fair chance of enduring . . . a process of moral and mental destruction. In no part of England have I seen such disgusting open-air performances as the hobbledehoys and wenches of the Fylde Coast enact in the lanes, in the shelters, on the sandhills during the season and, for that matter, out of it.

It is no uncommon thing to see a woman standing drinks for men they favour, men of a type that would have been under police supervision in London or our chief cities. The truth is, by far the greater number of people who patronize Blackpool go there not for the ozone but for the orgies that are part and parcel of the 'outing'.

It is a place where the unsuspicious stranger might undergo some of those experiences fondly believed to be confined to peculiar quarters of London if he be not careful.

Undoubtedly, this was a wild exaggeration—to the point of total fabrication and clearly designed for a particular readership. All the same, the image of the brazen hussy of the Lancashire Coast was to be Blackpool's albatross for many a long, successful, year. The average Northerner on holiday there took a harder-headed view. The morality, or lack of it, he could cope with; what he was suspicious of was Blackpool's equally hard-headed approach to money, the 'we have to live in the winter when you've gone' syndrome. The faint-hearted (or less strong-willed) went to Southport or Morecambe!

If Blackpool smarted under *John Bull's* criticism it didn't show—and 1909 was a bumper season. After all, it was the hobbledehoys and wenches, the virtuous young women and the well-brought up youths who provided Blackpool with the where-withal to live—and the fat to live on during the bleak winter months. *John Bull* didn't!

14 Blackpool's South Shore

Gypsy lore, hard fact and a dream of a White City

Blackpool's South Shore had always felt itself a somewhat separate community. Consciously or unconsciously it fostered its own identity, feeling itself remote from the seat of power 'up North' in Talbot Square. The South Shore's pier, the Victoria, was built at the very edge of the town and it was the end of the line for the promenade trams for forty years.

The 'inland' tramway route was built parallel to the Promenade in the mid 1890s and shortly afterwards a link was established with St Annes and Lytham. When this system was electrified a peculiar system was employed—central poles down the middle of the road rather than span-wires. This meant that there was very little clearance between the trams and the poles which in turn meant that the cars had to be fitted with mesh guards on their open top decks to prevent South Shoreite heads coming into contact with the poles. In turn, this prompted a South Shore Councillor to comment: 'The cages on the trams are only fit for a menagerie. The Council must think we are wild beasts.'

Blackpool had doubled its population in the 1890s, but none of this development had been on the seafront south of the Victoria Pier. Bearing in mind that the borough boundary to the north was only a little way up the cliffs from the Gynn Inn, if further development was to take place it would have to be on the sandhills between South Shore and Squires Gate.

A correspondent to the Blackpool *Gazette* was to comment:

My opinion is that South Shore will remain stationary until something is done in the way of Promenade extensions further South. There is a healthy demand for plots of land upon which to build a smaller and less expensive type of sea-fronting residential house; and if the Promenade could be extended as far as Squires Gate it would mean an immense increase in the rateable value of the town and would bring the better type of residents who cannot at present secure a sea-fronting house without the expenditure of a large sum of money.

The land the correspondent had in mind was a substantial tract of wind-blown sandhills stretching a mile or more to the southern borough boundary and inland as far as the railway and Lytham Road. Just beyond the Victoria Pier was the infant Pleasure Beach, an encampment of gypsies and little else; developing it would, indeed, add substantially to Blackpool's sea-front—and, as the correspondent dutifully pointed out, its rateable value.

Gypsies had been a part of Blackpool life for many years. Ned Boswell had come to the town in the 1830s, to be followed in the 1860s and '70s by the Lees and Young families, then the Greys, Herons and Franklins. It is suggested that the latter families at least, came from East Anglia—George Borrow country. The date is surely significant—the traumatic mid-Victorian years when the traditional way of life gave way to the steam and iron of the industrial society.

At first, the gypsies settled on the northern cliffs and a visit to the palmist or clairvoyant was an essential part of a Blackpool holiday. The most famous, by far, was Sarah Boswell—the original Gypsy Sarah no doubt who lived to a ripe old age (legend has it the full century, others suggest ninety-two). She was buried in the Corporation Cemetery and was possibly the first gypsy to be interred in one. But in keeping with tradition her van and personal possessions were burned.

The spread of housing along the northern cliffs forced a move to the sandhills south of the South Shore and here, advertising themselves as 'Gipsy Sarah's Only Daughter in England' and 'Gipsy Sarah's Eldest Clever Granddaughter' the family continued to ply their trade. Around them grew up a collection of coconut shies, penny games, and even a miniature railway. It was the beginning of the massive amusement park to become known as the Pleasure Beach.

In 1904 the first permanent structure appeared on the Pleasure Beach site—'Sir Hiram Maxim's Captive Flying Machine'. It was a giant version of the chair-plane roundabout with gondolas in place of the usual chairs. This was, after all, less than a year since Wilbur and Orville Wright had achieved powered flight. The ride survived several changes of design (at one time it sported rocketships) and has now been restored to its original condition and has regained its original title!

So far as the South Shore residents were concerned, the gypsies were a mixed blessing; the well-to-do in their villas along Lytham road were always aware of the tented encampment between them and the sea. The gypsies might be colourful characters and an undoubted attraction to the holidaymakers but they were also dubious characters, not averse to a little petty pilfering from the property around.

An unfortunate occurence involving one of these well-to-do villas sparked off the final move to have the gypsies removed from the sandhills. A correspondent (sheltering, no doubt wisely under the pseudonym 'South Shoreite') wrote to the local paper reporting that a gypsy had been caught by a guard dog whilst attempting to steal from 'a respectable home' in Lytham road; later the dog had been found on the railway line with its head severed. It is quite likely, of course, that the dog was decapitated by a passing Lancashire & Yorkshire locomotive, but so far as 'South Shoreite' was concerned the gypsies were to blame.

On 4 December 1908 the *Gazette* observed:

> Blackpool is quite in the fashion in regard to people and politics. Europe is worrying itself about a little handful of people on the Balkan peninsula, South Africa is much concerned in an attempt to evict Indian labour and so on. Blackpool's problem is centered on the gipsy encampment among the sandhills at the South Shore.

Typically, Blackpool was finding its proper place in world affairs; it was determined at least not to be left out. The editorial goes on, with much setting apart of possibly unorthodox phrases in quotation marks:

> The gipsy has always been 'The Monarch of all he surveys' down there. Perhaps attracted to the sandy shore at first by the free life of the tent and caravan, carrying with it the freedom from rent and rates he was quick to find it was a 'happy hunting ground' for the 'pieces of silver' with which the visitors were very willing to 'cross' their sunburned palms, in return for a little soothsaying.

Three days later the rival *Blackpool Times* joined the battle:

> There may be some lamentations at the disappearance of a picturesque tribe with whom is associated a certain amount of romance, but these will not be heard at South Shore. Those who live nearest to them will have fewest regrets . . .
>
> Gypsy lore is all very well and as presented by George Borrow is extremely fascinating, but romance flies out of the window when the gypsy steals into the larder—or carries off your faithful house-dog to die an awful death.

The correspondent to the newspaper who had pointed out the advantage of developing the sandhills stepped neatly round the problem of the establishment of the Pleasure Beach by pointing out:

> There may be some difficulty owing to the development of the Pleasure Beach, but owners will be sufficiently wide awake when the time comes to make best use of the land for building purposes and a sort of White City, properly enclosed will very likely be evolved out of this somewhat crude type of pleasure ground.

All of which brought it down to the gypsies! The result was a bye-law which stated:

> No gypsy tent, shed, caravan or encampment shall be permitted on any part of the land set apart as a Fair Ground (except with the written consent of the Corporation) . . . and no person following the calling of clairvoyant, phrenologist, palmist or quack doctor, or any person pretending or professing to tell fortunes or use any subtle craft, means or device by palmistry or otherwise, to deceive or impose on any of His Majesty's subjects shall be permitted on any part of the land set aside as a Fair Ground.

Although in principle limited to the fair ground area, this regulation effectively removed the gypsies from the immediate South Shore. The *Gazette* commented wryly:

> . . . one cannot keep from asking why a 'clairvoyant, phrenologist, palmist or quack doctor' should be barred here whilst others in the 'upper circles' of the town are allowed to practice subtle craft and flourish on it.

In 1910, on St Valentine's Day to be precise, an eviction order was served on the South Shore gypsies. But it wasn't as simple as that. The last family did not leave until 1926, just about the time when, after the construction of the massive New South Promenade the tract of land became available for development. Appropriately the Boswells were the last to go; even then it was simply a move up the promenade (and possibly up-market) to the Golden Mile.

There they have survived the development. Gypsy 'clairvoyants, phrenologists and palmists' (if not quack doctors) are part of the new, glittering Golden Mile and if anyone should try to move them from their concrete and plastic vardos there they will be able to call for help from, it seems, every international star who ever did a summer season in Blackpool!

15 Blackpool Promenade

Towards the Seven Golden Miles, inland to the park and upwards to the skies

The Blackpool Improvement Act of 1917 empowered the Corporation to construct:

> . . . a promenade on or adjoining the foreshore and comprising a carriage drive, footways, promenade, sea wall and embankment, commencing at the southerly terminus of the existing promenade and terminating at the southerly boundary of the Borough.
>
> A sea-water swimming bath situated on the foreshore on the western side of the existing promenade and adjacent thereto.
>
> A promenade or parade on the foreshore with a sea wall or embankment on the westerly side thereof, commencing at the northerly boundary of the existing borough extending in a northerly direction for a distance of 1 mile 1 furlong or thereabouts and terminating at a point opposite to Arundel Avenue.
>
> A public walk or promenade between the Blackpool and Fleetwood Tramroad and the foreshore commencing at the northern boundary of the existing borough and terminating at a point opposite to the southerly boundary wall of the Norbreck Hydro.
>
> A sea-water swimming bath situated on the foreshore on the westerly side and adjacent . . .

In effect, these works would extend the Blackpool Promenade to $5\frac{1}{2}$ miles, with only $1\frac{1}{2}$ left to go to the magic 'Seven Golden Miles'. In practical terms they doubled its length and involved massive sea-defence works as well as road building.

Until 1917, when the Bispham Urban District was absorbed into the Blackpool Borough, the Promenade had ended at a point just north of the Gynn; the sea-front parade and sea wall from there to North Pier had been built in two stages—the majority in 1899 and the short section round the seaward side of the Metropole Hotel (Princess Parade) in 1912. The northerly extension would carry the

137

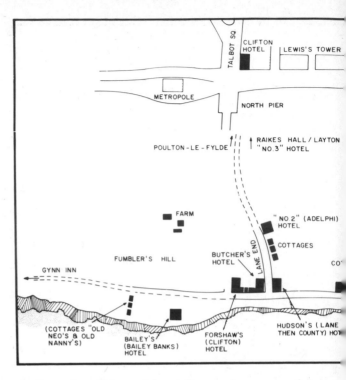

sea-front parade from the old boundary well past the centre of the road fronting the sea at Bispham.

That road (on the landward side of the tramroad) already existed as far as Norbreck Hydro. The 'public walk or promenade' between the tramroad and the foreshore was not built, except for a short section from the old borough boundary to Uncle Tom's Cabin. From that point on the cliff-top was left in more or less its natural state. The sea-water swimming bath did not materialise as such; it became the boating lake at the Cabin.

The works to the north, it was anticipated, would help to stabilise the eroding cliffs (it was only ten years before that the old Uncle Tom's Cabin had tumbled into the sea); incorporating Bispham gave Blackpool ample development land along the cliff-top. The parade at shore level was to be a massive affair, backed by artificial 'rockery' in concrete to hold back the crumbling grass-faced cliffs. Bispham might have been content to lose a field's length of land in sixty years. Blackpool didn't intend to lose an inch if it could help it!

The southerly extension was a logical one—straight down from

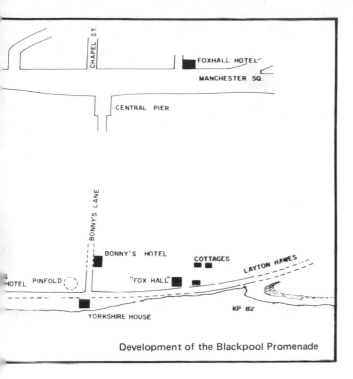

CHAPEL ST

FOXHALL HOTEL
MANCHESTER SQ.

CENTRAL PIER

BONNY'S LANE

BONNY'S HOTEL

COTTAGES

LAYTON HAWES

HOTEL   PINFOLD

"FOX HALL"

KP 82

YORKSHIRE HOUSE

Development of the Blackpool Promenade

the Victoria Pier past the Pleasure Beach to the borough boundary
at Starr Gate. The sandhills posed few problems and the sea wall
was built well 'forward' of the natural high-water mark. The area
reclaimed was substantial with ample room for a sea-front parade,
gardens, footways and tramway reservation between the shore and
the Promenade; from sea-wall to existing railway line was the best
part of five hundred yards. On this new land were laid out avenues
with solid sounding names—Walpole, Napier, Bentinck and
Raleigh. A new road parallel to and inland from the Promenade
continued the line, and the name, of Clifton Drive coming in over
the boundary from Lytham St Annes.

The first sea-front works completed after World War I were not,
in fact, the new extensions but a rebuilding of the North Promenade
between Princess Parade and the Gynn. This road was itself barely
a quarter-century old, built to circle the private Claremont Park of
the 1860s. The rebuilt promenade, opened in 1924, was a magnificent affair in three tiers, two broad parades below a colonnaded
covered walkway and atop it all the tramway moved from the side of

the old road on to its own reservation.

Work was proceeding all the while on the major extensions to north and south and names were beginning to be something of a problem. Blackpool already had a South, Central and North Promenade and a Princess Parade, so what should be the name of the new extensions? To the north they are Royal indeed—Princess Parade leads to the North Promenade, which leads to Empress Drive which leads to Queens Promenade which gives way to Prince's Parade (the final mile or so the Cleveleys boundary and not built until the late thirties). The southern extensions was not so regally titled. It had to be content to be simply the New South Promenade.

Other improvements were scheduled for the 1920s and this time inland—a move to take the visitors away from the crowded seafront. On the eastern edge of the town the corporation laid out a park—but a park the town could be proud of in its Jubilee year. 30,000 roses were to bloom there, there were Italian gardens, a woodland garden, a vast boating lake, fountains, colonnades and loggias, an eighteen-hole golf course, two putting greens, hard and grass tennis courts and bowling greens—flat and, naturally, this being North and the home of the Waterloo Cup—crown. Above all, crown. The whole 250 acres was pinpointed by a spectacular clock-tower (a tribute to one of the town's great Victorian entrepreneurs Alderman Cocker) named Stanley—a tribute to the even greater Lancastrian name of the Earls of Derby.

It was a typical grand gesture, but not an unqualified success. It was away from the bustling brawny sea-front, away, even from the tram routes and for a time the Corporation ran a curious half-tram half-bus vehicle labelled 'To and from the New Park'. Legend has it that visitors were disorientated by the quiet of the park and suspicious of a free facility in a town where one expected to pay for everything. (The fact is that for years the Tower building advertised its ordinary lifts 'free lift' in letters two feet high; the Tower Ascent was a different matter and not to be confused!)

Stanley Park was proposed as the site for an 'aerodrome' and this was decidedly not a success, in spite of its promotion by Sir Alan Cobham. The first aerodrome, established many years before had been on the sandhills at Squires Gate; an air pageant had been held there as early as 1909, the same year that Bleriot flew the Channel. An exhibition of 'aeronautical skill' was given during that summer by Hubert Latham—typically, in a gale. Flying came into its own that year. Henry Farman set up a record by flying 144 miles in just over four and a half hours, Paulhan set altitude records, Wright demonstrated flying before Edward VII and air races were held on Doncaster Racecourse.

The following year Paulhan won the *Daily Mail* prize for a flight from London to Manchester and there was a full-scale 'flying carnival' at Squires Gate. Already there was a Lancashire Aero Club and the case for a permanent aerodrome was being pressed—possibly inside a race course or on a golf course.

Flying continued at Squires Gate for many years and in the twenties and early thirties stunt flying was a popular attraction. It is said that the Corporation was influenced by Cobham (whose Flying Circus was a regular visitor to the town) when selecting Stanley Park as the site for an aerodrome but it is equally possible that they were influenced by the fact that Squires Gate was not technically in Blackpool but over the boundary in Lytham St Annes.

Eventually, the flyers moved back to Squires Gate and, on the outbreak of World War II it was taken over by the RAF and a little later on they were joined by a detachment of the Free Polish Airforce.

It was from Squires Gate, in January 1941 that the pioneer aviator Amy Johnson took off on what was her last flight; her Oxford trainer aircraft crashed in the Thames estuary. Then, at the end of the war, civil flying was resumed and Blackpool Airport was established—albeit in Lytham St Annes. Flights to the Isle of Man were resumed and at one time there was an extensive network of scheduled services.

Remote, though, from the main network, Blackpool Airport retains a particular atmosphere—casual, even informal. Here there is none of the nerve-racking hustle of Heathrow or Kennedy (and even Ringway seems frenetic in comparison). Passengers take the bus—at one time the Lytham road tram—to the airport or go by car. Parking is easy (if the main car park is closed there's always room behind one of the spruced-up wartime prefabs). The main terminal building is single-storey and it's only a short walk across the apron to the waiting Air UK fifty-seater about to hop across to the Isle of Man. Likely as not, returning passengers will take the coach from the regular stop outside, joining the happy daytrippers on their way back to the East Lancashire towns. Flying may have opened up the world (and beyond), Pan Am and Concorde may be fighting for the North Atlantic hordes, but Blackpool still provides the most convenient way of hopping across to the Isle of Man!

16 Blackpool's Heyday

The New South Promenade. Mayfair and Broadway. Tin Pan Alley and the Wonder Wurlitzer

On his inauguration as Mayor of Blackpool in 1927 Alderman Robert Fenton suggested that for the next few years 'Financial zeal should be tempered with economy.' The town, he suggested, should 'call a halt to its programme of public expenditure except for such improvement schemes as are already in hand and other urgent matters, such as the housing problem'. Blackpool, Alderman Fenton pointed out, had 'scarcely had breathing space between completing one big scheme and projecting another'. With advantage to the ratepayer and without injuring the town's reputation as a holiday resort he felt they could 'Rest a bit and enjoy what we have got.'

Fenton's statement, hedged about as it was with provisos and exceptions, was bound to be popular with the hard-pressed ratepayers but the simple fact was that, thanks to the frenzy of activity during the previous years, Blackpool had enough sea-front development land to last it for the next half-century! They could, indeed, sit back and enjoy the benefits.

Fenton was surely the archetypal Blackpool business man. In his time he had been a grocer, sub-postmaster, brick-maker, entertainment proprietor (he owned the Hippodrome Theatre for a time) and was a well-known local builder. He'd seen the population increase six-fold in his lifetime, double in twenty-five years; it was now approaching the magic figure of 100,000. In 1926, there were 473 trains a day coming into Blackpool, bringing a total of 2,209,000 visitors to the town. Admittedly, the General Strike had curtailed that season somewhat ('The holiday purse was somewhat restricted', the Year Book commented); all the same, the tramways were contributing a healthy £175,000 a year to the rates!

1926 had seen the golden jubilee of Blackpool's incorporation as a Borough, work was proceeding on the sea-front extensions and both

143

the New South Promenade and Stanley Park were officially opened by the Earl of Derby in October that year. One Alderman was knighted and three were made Freemen of the Borough. Two of them had spread Blackpool's name far and wide—Lindsay Parkinson of the construction firm and W. H. Broadhead, owner of the chain of North of England Variety Theatres.

After an unsuccessful attempt to replace the autumn Illuminations by a carnival (in 1923 and 1924) the Corporation had seen the error of its ways and revived them for the 1925 season. The special jubilee 'Lights' were switched on on 25 September 1926—and promptly switched off again three days later when the Council was informed that they were in breach of the government regulations still in force as a result of the General Strike of May.

Opening the new promenade extension was one thing—developing it was another. At the last minute there had been a change of emphasis after a councillor, W. D. Halstead had suggested (at a meeting of the South Shore Traders' Association) that boarding houses rather than private dwellings should be erected. It was to be a number of years before anything was built on the new promenade—and when it *was* built it was neither boarding house nor private villa.

Once again a name bubbles to the surface, this time that of Mrs Maud Bourne. She, above all, conceived the idea of medium-sized select hotels, carried the concept through and thereby created something unique. Brighton might have its Regency terraces, Douglas its splendid curving bay of matching Victorian facades, Blackpool would have the contemporary equivalent.

The New South Promenade, separated from the hurly-burly of the town by the Pleasure Beach has a very special atmosphere. No slot palace, burger bar or ice-cream parlour intrudes on the curving line of the Bourne Crescent hotels. The style is neo-classical, dentilled pediments, tympana, sometimes flanked by decorative urns, ivory faience set off by a background of russet brick. The details echo the features in the gardens between the Promenade and the sea—colonnades, arches topped by broken pediments, urn-topped columns—all the paraphernalia of a Graeco-Roman fantasy. It could be overpowering (at best), pretentious at worst, but somehow it isn't. It is scaled for the human being. The columns flank and the colonnade shields a children's paddling pool and the hotels, however large (and they are not very large) are well-to-do domestic, not jet-settingly uniform, idiosyncratic—as the human species is.

The names are evocative of the period. Blackpool ran out of names like 'Grand', 'Imperial' 'Queens' and 'Savoy' half a century before so here are the New Mayfair, Waldorf, Broadway, Arandora Star, Warwick, Colwyn and, of course New Esplanade and, naturally, Bourne. The Red Court is just round the corner, facing south over the Harrowside green; the Windsor Court is round the corner again in Clifton Drive, alongside the St Clement and the Scotia—across the road are the Russell and the Royal. All are a far cry from the lodging houses and boarding houses of the older part of the town.

To the north of the Gynn the fantasy begins again. The style is similar, possibly a little more powerful, the size perhaps a little larger, the titles interchangeable—Boston, Berkeley, Commodore, Westmorland, New Cumberland, New Continental. For the columns and colonnades and gardens of the south read the clifftop greensward and neo-classical lift tower down to the North Shore boating pool, echoing the paddling pool at Harrowside.

Blackpool has always disclaimed any reputation for architectural or environmental excellence. It does itself a disservice, for the developments of the twenties and thirties are well-judged and well-crafted, spirited but not over-exuberant; *mature* is the word. The New South Promenade is particularly successful; it has a harmony and a unity. If 'fitness for purpose' is an ideal, then here the ideal becomes reality—or very nearly. That fantasy is part of the attraction after all, and one would not be surprised to see Evelyn Laye waltz, singing, out of a promenade shelter or a chorus line from *Gold Diggers of 1933* come high-kicking out of the Broadway!

The twenties and thirties are often referred to as Blackpool's heyday, and certainly in these days the resort was as successful as it has ever been. The Very Top Names in entertainment played a summer season at Blackpool automatically. Couples foxtrotted or Palais-glided seemingly for ever to the magnificent swelling sounds of the Wonder Wurlitzer in the Tower Ballroom. The candy-floss was never stickier, the fish-batter never crisper, the chips so abundant or the beer so powerful. There was a score of live shows, a dozen cinemas, a hundred or more fish and chip shops, three hundred or more ice-cream parlours, three thousand hotels, boarding houses and lesser establishments, all competing with each other—and the Great Depression.

The Golden Mile was never so raucous, the Fat Ladies never fatter. Visitors could peep at 'the Starving Honeymoon Couple' for a penny a time—and did, in their thousands. The Rector of Stiffkey, exhibited himself in a barrel—a real coup for the showman who imported him from Norfolk. The song pluggers in the open-fronted music parlours pounded out the latest novelty numbers hour after hour, copies at 6d each passing over to willing hands after each performance. Signboards on the road to Blackpool advertised Lawrence Wright (Horatio Nicholls, known as 'the Father of Tin Pan Alley')—simply and directly: '6 miles to Lawrence Wright', they proclaimed.

George Formby made his first appearance at the Palace Theatre in 1921, desperately trying to find a personality unlike his too-famous Father. Sandy Powell was topping the bill. Blackpool got its own waxworks in 1929—a Tussaud's to rival London's, but firmly labelled 'Louis Tussaud's'. 'Doodles' was the clown at the Tower Circus and Reginald Dixon and Howard Finch were at the organs in the Tower and the Winter Gardens. The talkies had come in 1929 and Gracie Fields had come to make 'Sing As We Go' in 1934.

In 1935 there were protests about the Golden Mile. 'An eyesore . . . the happy hunting ground of penny gaffs'. An Improvement Act was brought in containing a clause prohibiting 'offensive and objectionable exhibitions of human persons'. It made little difference—this was the boozy, bosomy, slap and tickle image of the town that clung to it, like uneaten fairy-floss, for a generation.

Blackpool cried all the way to the bank! The same year it introduced the first of a brand new generation of streamlined tramcars, added the 'Grand National' (Britain's only twin-track roller coaster) to the Pleasure Beach, approved a £300,000 drainage scheme for Anchorsholme and Little Bispham and saw plans

South Promenade, Blackpool

approved to rebuild the Manchester Hotel at a cost of £30,000. More hotels were finished, a new market approved, new road-building schemes introduced. And this was in the depths of the Depression, in a town not due to celebrate its diamond jubilee until the following year.

Ramsay MacDonald had opened the municipal aerodrome at Stanley Park in 1931, a suitably controversial figure in view of the arguments over it which rumbled on through the 1930s. The following year a Councillor Jacob Parkinson resigned the chairmanship of what was said to be 'the intensely disliked municipal aerodrome'—and the 'Graf Zepplin' flew over the town. There was stunt flying; the Flying Circus came to town—and gave the town a spectacular air crash. The following year one of the Isle of Man planes gave it another. It was all part and parcel of the life of the 1930s—as were the fires.

147

Fires there were—in profusion. Each one seems to have been greater than the last and some seemed hardy annuals. One entrepreneur, it was whispered, could tell you when his next would be!

Everybody who was anybody—and millions who were nobodies—danced and fried their way through those heady summers. Larry Gains, the Canadian boxer, Laurel and Hardy and Sir Harry Lauder were all in Blackpool in the same month in 1932. Even 1939, with the clouds of war welling up on the horizon there were massive improvements in hand. There was a new pavilion for the North Pier (to replace one destroyed in one of the inevitable spectacular fires), the Casino at the Pleasure Beach—to replace the 'Monte Carlo Rococo' of the earlier one, new swimming baths to the north, a new solarium at Harrowside to the south. Roads were being widened, sewers expanded, an Odeon was rising and a completely new Opera House (the largest auditorium outside London and in a style more suited to an Odeon than a Covent Garden) was ready for opening.

The population was well over 100,000 and pushing on towards 150,000, yet there was still land for building on. The big dipper still swooped, the passengers still screamed delightedly and dutifully, the donkeys still plodded and jingled their way on the central beach. Britain might be off the Gold Standard but the Seven Golden Miles boiled on.

17 Blackpool Pleasure Beach I

The Velvet Coaster, the Spectatorium and the man from Chicago

Even before the gypsies were moved off the sandhills at South Shore the Pleasure Beach had begun to develop. From 1905 to 1909 a miniature railway (the first of its kind) ran on the dunes. Appropriately, one station was called 'Gipsyville' and it was close by the traditional domed tent home of 'Gipsy Sarah's Eldest Clever Grand-daughter'. Maxim's Flying Machine appeared in 1904 and there was a crude 'switchback'. In 1906 a scenic railway was built (the first in Europe) and this survived until 1934.

Very soon the Pleasure Beach also had 'River Caves of the World', a water chute, motor track, the 'Gee Whizz', the 'Katzenjammer Kastle' and many other attractions. Then, in 1909, Blackpool got a visit from a Mr Strickler, an employee of the Federal Constructing Company of Chicago. They had built the first switchback in the world, at Coney Island, in 1884, and the first water chute in the world for the Chicago World's Fair. The second had been at the Earl's Court exhibition in London in 1900 and the third in New York, so Blackpool's wasn't the first for once. However, Blackpool was to get a new attraction for the 1909 season, courtesy of Mr Strickler.

The *Gazette* welcomed him to Blackpool on 23 February:

> A newcomer in our midst this weekend who was taking in the great things of Blackpool with a quiet observant eye is Mr Strickler, who has come all the way from Chicago. He is interested in another Pleasure Beach novelty promised for the coming season—the Velvet Coaster.

'Ariel', a columnist in the same paper commented on Mr Strickler:

> Mr Strickler is an American, yet different from the usual type we get over here in the entertainment line, being quiet and modest and presumably that is why he has such a high appreciation of the British character—as I found he had.

The Velvet Coaster—the first true 'roller coaster'—was ready for the summer season (eighteen weeks in 1909) and the *Blackpool Herald* described a ride on it:

> . . . a huge and extensive construction over which you fly in velvet upholstered cars of a motor-car type, with comfort and ease, which gives the sensation of gliding through the air off terra firma. It is the latest development of the switchback known to science. Up and down mountains you go at a terrific pace and in perfect safety. It is an exhilarating experience. You do not run on rails. There is no iron on the track, but the wheels run on maple and that is the secret of the velvety sensation. Indeed, it is like coasting down a hill in the most luxurious of motor cars.

Travelling fairs, with their roundabouts and swing-boats were common and still appear up and down the country from time to time; amusement parks in connection with major exhibitions seem inevitable also—the Chicago World's Fair, Earl's Court, the Franco-British Exhibition in 1908 (which brought the reference to 'White City' from the resident complaining about the gypsies on the South Shore) and so on. Every seaside resort in the country developed a funfair of some kind, but Blackpool Pleasure Beach always had a bigger one, a better one—or got it first!

Strickler was in Blackpool at the invitation of Messrs Outhwaite and Bean, the owners of the Pleasure Beach, and the construction of the Velvet Coaster marked the beginning of a long association. The newspaper columnist who observed at this time, 'Messrs Bean and Outhwaite must have exhausted America in the matter of novelties and it looks as if they will have to leave the Far West for next year's surprises and exploit the Far East', was anticipating events; America was to influence the Pleasure Beach for many, many many years to come.

The 'surprise' for the 1910 season was the Naval Spectatorium, described as being:

> . . . somewhat like a theatre, and as you sit . . . you have put before you the most realistic spectacular ever devised. The theme is the historic battle of Chesapeke [sic] Bay between the 'Monitor' and the 'Merrimac' and the audience witness this engagement as though actually at the scene. Water effects, sun set, moon rise etc. are all astonishingly imitated by ingenious electrical contrivances.

Finally we are shown the South Coast of England off Spithead where ranges in Review Order the Channel Squadron.

Clearly, the reporter who wrote this was impressed; the 'electrical contrivances' were superior to the hand-cranked film camera of the period.

John William Outhwaite died the following year, but Bean went on, developing, often with Strickler, what was to become Europe's Greatest Pleasure park. And films, more importantly film-*making*, came to the Pleasure Beach in 1920. Visitors could take part in productions in an open-air studio on the Pleasure Beach and could see the film they had taken part in at the Casino Cinema later in the week. Local newsreels were a positive part of cinema fare in these pre-sound days, but feature films were something different! Among the staff on hand to help in the making of these 'Pro-Am' films was a Mr William Adler, who had been connected with the making of D. W. Griffith's epic *Birth of A Nation*. Nothing less than the best for Blackpool Pleasure Beach!

The Virginia Reel (now known simply as 'the Reel' and the survivor of several changes of background scenery) appeared in 1922, the same year as the Noah's Ark. The Big Dipper, then thought to be the ultimate in roller coasters (65ft high, cars travelling at 30mph) was constructed in 1923 and added to the scenic railway and the Velvet Coaster. In September 1924 the Velvet Coaster ('substantially built', the local press pointed out) was blown down by a gale—but re-erected; the Pleasure Beach wasn't going to lose one of its most popular attractions. In fact, some years later it actually moved the whole thing; rebuilt and renamed it survives—in essence at least—as the roller coaster (simply that!) today.

In the 1920s, the Pleasure Beach was still at 'the end of the line'; trams coming in from the north carried the destination 'Pleasure Beach' (guaranteed free advertising the length and breadth of the Promenade!) and terminated there as they had done since the old conduit line had been built in 1885.

Times, however, were a-changing. The Corporation had taken over the Blackpool & Fleetwood Tramroad and there was now a through service from Fleetwood along the Promenade to the

Pleasure Beach. The Blackpool Improvement Act of 1917 had empowered the town to construct extensions to the sea-front north and south (bringing the goal of a new 'South of South Shore' development nearer) and by 1923 the effects were beginning to be felt. Across the road from the Casino building rose the Open Air Baths built in a clear white faience and in a severely classical style quite unlike that of the Monte Carlo Rococo of the Casino.

Compared to it, the Pleasure Beach was a bizarre collection of architectural styles—alongside the Rococo was Venetian, oriental, funfair and frankly 'free style'. The features on the new South Promenade, then the first hotels, confirmed the trend; the Blackpool of the thirties was going to be coolly classical.

William George (by then Alderman) Bean died in 1929 and his son-in-law Leonard Thompson took over the running of the Pleasure Beach. He had been concerned with the business for some years and, like all such showmen had travelled widely, visiting similar enterprises. In 1922 he had been to the British Exhibition at Wembley and had noticed the work of Joseph Emberton, who had designed some of the pavilions. He met him, possibly by chance, and shortly after he took over the Pleasure Beach, invited Emberton to visit Blackpool.

Once again, the particular chemistry of a partnership took over. As Strickler had collaborated with Bean and brought the new attractions to the Pleasure Beach, Emberton and Thompson combined to give it a new face. In doing so, they gave Blackpool—and Britain—some of its most exciting buildings ever. And not in the respectable Graeco-Roman of the New South Promenade either; theirs was an entirely 'modern' style, happy-go-lucky, frolicsome, 'liking to be beside the seaside' using steel, glass and concrete (and sun and light and air) in a way that was new—breathtakingly new—and never to be repeated.

Reviewing his work in Blackpool for the architectural press a journalist remarked on Emberton's 'spirit of buffoonery' and the 'enthusiasm and eccentricity in the eye of the beholder'. It would have been easier to say it was simply the Architecture of Pleasure.

18 Blackpool Pleasure Beach II

The Fun House and the Grand National. The Casino and Joseph Emberton. Above all, Leonard Thompson

The happy chance that brought Leonard Thompson of the Blackpool Pleasure Beach Company and Joseph Emberton, architect, together at the British Exhibition at Wembley resulted in an association every bit as fruitful and exciting as that involving Outhwaite, Bean and Strickler twenty-five years before.

Thompson was in charge of an amusement park which was undoubtedly successful but aesthetically something of a nightmare; Emberton was a first-class architect with a number of prestige commissions to his name. Bringing them together—one a thrusting young businessman with a background of Blackpool's bouncing showbiz, the other an essentially 'London' man, a modernist architect who had designed the HMV Building in Oxford Street, Simpson's of Piccadilly and the Empire Hall at Olympia—could (by all the rules *should*) have produced the shortest partnership ever! Instead it produced a unique relationship that was to give Thompson's Empire of Enjoyment a sophisticated new image and inspire Emberton to produce some of the most exciting structures of the decade.

Joseph Emberton was born in Staffordshire in 1889. After Art School at Newcastle under Lyme he won a scholarship to the Royal College of Art. The two years he spent there were, he said, the dullest of his life. However, he made the acquaintance of Thomas Tait who was to teach him, he insisted, everything he should have learned at college.

He began his career in the offices of Trehearne & Norman, then working on office buildings for the new Kingsway, then being pushed through the tangle of narrow streets between the Strand and Holborn. Pevsner said of the Kodak Building there, 'Here is an early example . . . of the treatment of a commercial building to which the future belonged.'

During Word War I Emberton served in the Army (which had found that architects could, unlike their own engineering draughtsmen, produce accuracy at speed) and on his return to civilian life worked with Tait on Adelaide House (on the City side of London Bridge, next to the church of St Magnus Martyr). This was in the office of Sir John Burnet, who had designed the Kodak building in Kingsway.

He was commissioned to design stands for the British Exhibition in 1926 at the instigation of Sir Lawrence Weaver and it was these which attracted Leonard Thompson's attention. From there he went on to a major commission—that of the Empire Hall at Olympia which introduced the German 'modernist' style to Great Britain.

In designing the Simpson building in Piccadilly, Emberton made a distinctive use of light as an integral part of architecture; primary colour lamps mixing to provide secondary colours illuminate the facade as an element of the design. His clubhouse for the Royal Corinthian Yacht Club won him the RIBA Bronze Medal— the first time it had been awarded for a 'modern' building.

Thompson invited him to Blackpool and commissioned him to re-shape some of the existing features on the Pleasure Beach and also to design some new ones. Each structure posed particular problems but offered exhilarating opportunities. Out went the imitative pastiche and the florid colouring and in came functional 'streamlined' modernity, flat white concrete facades emphasising the clear bright seaside light, sweeping curved canopies supported on slim metal columns, soaring art-deco towers with exaggerated fins throwing deep shadows or framing vast sky-reflecting glass facades.

Everything was light, sun, fresh air and, above all, *fun*. His station building for the miniature railway (1933) is no Victorian evocation. It is a simple 'back wall' and cantilevered roof—the most direct and functional answer to the problem. And across the way is the terminal feature for the re-sited Velvet Coaster—a concrete and glass box suspended over the curved track leading from the loading platform to the powered incline. It is direct, straightforward and eye-catching.

The facade for the Fun House (1934) gave him the opportunity to show what modernism could do. The only functional requirement was a rectangular central aperture—a balcony overlooking the walkway outside. So the rest was plain, white, texture provided by a horizontally finned feature at one side balancing a long slim canopy over the ground floor entrance.

Inside, he was required to provide balconies and staircases round a huge open glass-roofed space. The attention to detail on the handrails and so on is as careful as it would have been (and indeed had been) in an exhibition hall. The Emberton personality is stamped on all parts of the Pleasure Beach—the same canopies (even on as simple a structure as a sales kiosk), the same 'thirtyish' colours—orange and electric blue against stark white.

With the building of the Grand National in 1934 he faced his most exciting challenge. The mechanics of the ride demanded that the 'competing' cars should load from a central platform (reached by a subway) then swing away from each other round diverging curves to meet and run parallel to the powered incline. Over the whole loading area Emberton built a slim heart-shaped canopy, topping it with a soaring finned central tower ending in a lantern. Aware of the architectural possibilities of light he outlined the whole feature in neon. It is altogether a masterly example of architecture tied firmly to function.

At about this time, the 'Noah's Ark' of 1922 was refurbished and Emberton brought in Metcalfe, who had designed the coinage for the Irish Free State, to design the animals which forever circled the rocking ark. Again, these animals appeared in a chunky art-deco form without any concessions to the nursery.

And then came the proposal to replace the rococo Casino building at the entrance to the Pleasure Beach. It is as if all the other structures had been practice sessions for this building—by far his most challenging commission. Here he would be on show to everyone—Pleasure Beach patron or not—on an open corner site and visible from every angle. The building had to express not only its purpose but the purpose of the Pleasure Beach and, as the headquarters of the Pleasure Beach Company itself, the status of the organisation. By now he knew Leonard Thompson and Thompson knew him. Both knew there could be no compromise, no half-measures, no corner cutting.

It was 1936. Modernism was established, the Pleasure Beach had a bright new face, new hotels were springing up in smart art-deco to the south, to the north the 'Seafield' hotel had an 'imitation Pleasure Beach style' facade planted on its Victorian framework. Odeons and Essoldos up and down the country were changing the urban street-scape, Morecambe had its Midland Hotel—a brilliant sea-front design the equal of anything Emberton had produced, Bexhill had its De La Warre pavilion and resorts all along the coast were erupting imitation Embertons. The Casino had to go that bit further and set the pattern for the 1940s.

The first drawings, produced in December 1936 show a simple two-storey circular structure with a soaring vane of a tower. The more elaborate tower was, it has been suggested, proposed by Leonard Thompson. The purpose of the building was to house the company's offices and a collection of cafés, restaurants and bars. Kitchens were sited in the middle of the building and were capable of contracting or expanding as traffic demanded.

The resulting building is certainly the most exciting building of its decade and one of the most exciting of the twentieth century. In a way it expresses the century—or what it ought to have been. It uses modern materials—glass, concrete and light—and essentially looks forward to the future. The curving glass facade is interrupted only by the 'trademark' tower feature and a necessary communicating staircase. Emberton placed this gently-curving stair proud of the main facade of the building and glassed it in uninterrupted from top to bottom, showing off the curve of the stair. He used natural light—the play of sun and cloud reflected on the facade and plain white neon to line the building out at night.

Construction of the Casino was not without its problems—even its tragedies; the whole structure was built on a concrete raft floated on silting sand. Emberton (who was assisted on this project by Halstead Best, architect for the New South Promenade development) was pushing contemporary technology to its limits. But the results were worth it. The building is elegant, sophisticated and, above all, mature. In the forty-odd years since it was completed it has hardly ever been imitated and never surpassed. The Festival Hall on London's South Bank did not appear until fifteen years after the first Casino designs and by comparison is mundane. imitative.

Emberton remained, as so many pioneers of modern architecture in Britain have remained, unrecognised during his lifetime and for a quarter century afterwards. Of his work on Blackpool Pleasure Beach the *Architectural Record* had said 'buffoonery takes on a new significance'. Viewed retrospectively this was grudging praise. 'Modernistic' architecture was, admittedly, imported from the continent and not an instinctive native fashion. In its continental form it was cold to the point of being clinical, uncompromising in the worst sense of the word.

Joseph Emberton took the abstract concept and humanised it, warmed it and gave it a smiling face. Jutting canopies were meant to shade and shelter as well as stimulate the eye and express form, glass was meant to—*just*—enclose, steel to –*just*– support. Like the great Victorian baroque Tower Ballroom the buildings on the Pleasure Beach display architecture usually reserved for a privileged minority. Here they are available—and welcome everyone.

Few of the structures remain exactly as Emberton designed them. His feature for the Big Dipper has disappeared completely as has his design for the River Caves. The exterior of the Fun House is sadly altered and the chunky animals round the Noah's Ark have been replaced. The feature for the Grand National is virtually unchanged.

The later additions and alterations to the Casino building have not improved it, but there are features which, one feels Emberton would have approved of. Most decidedly he would have disapproved of the welter of colour and advertising on the face of the building and he may have viewed the prospect of running a monorail round his curving facade with little enthusiasm. Possibly—but only possibly—he might have approved of the glass capsule lift rising up the external face of the tower.

19 The Thirties

The advancement of science on the Pleasure Beach. The protecting male and the investigating reporter

The attraction of the amusement park ride is as difficult to explain as a sense of humour. The uninterested cannot understand why people should allow themselves to be hurled up and down, turned round and round (and these days over and over) and pay for the experience. Yet the average seeker of sensation can drift on to the dedicated enthusiast—an admittedly small minority—who can compare ride with ride, funfair with funfair, even type with type. The most dedicated *aficionados* can 'grade' roller coasters; some travel the world visiting amusement parks, some insist that only the traditionally timber built roller coaster is a *real* roller coaster able to give the absolutely correct experience.

In the amusement ride science has been wedded to mechanics to produce nothing more substantial than a sensation and the result can be developed in a multitude of forms. But the end product whatever its form is ephemeral. The product can please the eye or simply be eye-catching. The motion is obvious but cannot be experienced except by participating, and the reason for participating remains obscure!

In 1936, Blackpool brought together two of its functions—pleasure resort and conference venue when the British Association for the Advancement of Science held its annual conference there and discussed (in a series of bizarre lectures and seminars) the motives for indulging in amusement rides.

Leonard Thompson was invited to present a paper to the Association Conference, 'The Amusement Park and its Machinery.' He began:

> I have felt inclined to dwell at length on the rides developed from the old switchback because not only are they the most spectacular we have

but also because with proper maintenance they have become the backbone of the whole Amusement Park for well over a generation.

Ordinary, regulation stuff, promising a satisfying, if not exactly electrifying hour or so in the conference hall. But the delegates were in for a surprise.

I should be pleased to extend an invitation to the Pleasure Beach . . . If those of you who have not got weak hearts would test the devices and convince yourselves how the great masses of people who visit us do get entertainment and thrills from these machines.

A group of the delegates accepted and the press coverage of their visit to the Pleasure Beach was voluminous—naturally. A group of eminent scientists letting their hair down on the funfair? The story was irresistible (as Thompson no doubt realised when he issued his invitation).

Professor Edrington-Green, C.B.E., seventy-two years old (and looking remarkably like Neville Chamberlain) 'merrily crashed about on the Dodgems' according to one newspaper and the reporter heard him whisper to a colleague, 'Science made this possible.' From the dodgems he moved to the Grand National where he 'removed his hat, clutched it, together with his umbrella in one hand (!) and held on tightly with the other'. And at the conclusion of the ride, 'The professor was the same impassive figure, excited yet searching for more exciting pursuits. "It was an experience", he coolly remarked.'

During the conference a Mr Frank C. Thomas presented a paper entitled 'Psychology of Mass Entertainment', with reference to the Pleasure Beach, 'where aggressive impulses are harmlessly diverted and enhance esteem.'

The newspaper reports of the paper are studded with eye-catching sub-headings (themselves designed to dig deep into the reader's psyche)—'Lure of Fear', 'Courtship', 'The Protecting Male'.

Analysing the psychology of the amusement park ride Thomas observed:

I take the view myself that most of the people who patronise some of the devices on the Pleasure Beach largely for the sake of the opportunity for mutual stimulation which they afford would, in their absence, provide each other with such stimulation anyway and it is not, therefore by any means wholly to the bad that brief public opportunities for such activities should be provided.

It is, however, to be added that, with a certain type of patron, these devices do seem capable of lending themselves on occasion to a perhaps un-natural acceleration of the preliminary stages of courtship.

It will not do for those with greater social opportunities to say of the Pleasure Beach in their most regal and Victorian manner 'We are not Amused' for they amuse themselves in ways, which, to the psychologist, are exactly compatible.

. . . Mill proprietor and millhand meet with complete democratic equality on the common ground of the nursery.

May I suggest, in conclusion, that civilized life inevitably imposes the necessity for some vicarious satisfaction of our innate propensities and that the Pleasure Beach seems to afford facilities for this (on a harmless if somewhat infantile level) to the masses that are denied it in other and more expressive fashion. To that extent the existence of the Pleasure Beach is at once explained and justified.

Condescending it may be, a devastating example of damning with faint praise (and surely revealing a subconscious riddled with class obsessions), but it reveals that he hadn't consulted Professor Edrington-Green CBE. Neither had he discussed his views with the unnamed Doctor of Medicine delegate who had reportedly said: 'Great stuff, what, Professor? And to think that for all these years I have been giving my patients liquid medicine!'

A week later (perhaps as a result of seeing the reports of the conference delegates' visit to the Pleasure Beach) the *Daily Mirror* sent its intrepid reporter David Walker up to Blackpool—no doubt treading warily in case he slipped off the edge of the world—to report back on what he found there.

Within an hour of my arrival a waitress at the hotel had asked me whether I was a Catholic, an old woman had enquired whether I had ever had rheumatism and a small child had mistaken me for 'Daddy'.

. . . you could live in London for weeks without anyone taking such a sympathetic interest in your affairs. It is this intense comradeship that makes Blackpool what it is—the friendliest place in Britain. It teaches London how to LIVE.

It is impossible to be lonely here. Hundreds of people try to 'Mother' you, however hard you try not to resist.

In London when I tread on a women's toes at dances they sigh and murmur 'Oh dear! Isn't it hot? Shall we sit down?' When I did it in the Tower Ballroom here she said 'Never mind, Luv! Pick your feet oop!'.

Looking back over the intervening traumatic decades it is easy to forget how lacking in knowledge the thirties generation was. 'Background' information on the manners of the country rather than its metropolitan centre was hard to come by. The North had its own newspapers (the *Daily Dispatch* for instance) and northern editions of the nationals; there was regional and national radio— rigidly controlled by John Reith, with extremely limited air-time and a decidedly middle-class accent all over the country.

Films were made in the North, but for local consumption only and the rest were based in London and again with what Northerners would call a 'cut-glass' accent. Something like eight years later a documentary-drama film was made about the beginnings of the Rochdale Pioneers' Co-operative movement where the actors (and particularly actresses) make what was obviously a calculated attempt at a regional accent—and fail dismally. 'Young' John Laurie—the archetypal Scotsman of 'Dad's Army' was cast as a Lancashire weaver—with *disastrous* results! It is one thing that they fail (it has happened many times since), but what is significant is that no one expected anything less than success!

The North had its own variety theatre and its own 'names'— Frank Randle, Norman Evans, Jimmy James—which did not travel well. In the reverse direction Max Miller was totally unsuccessful north of Birmingham. The North still had its own separate identity totally incomprehensible to the South—which meant nationally. Gracie Fields (and possibly George Formby) alone bridged the gap, and then only when they became big star attractions. Is it sheer coincidence that the British Association for the Advancement of Science, Frank C. Thomas and David Walker started paying attention to Blackpool the year after *Sing As We Go* was released?

In *Sing As We Go* Gracie Fields played a mill-girl who, when 'th'mill' closed because of the Depression went to Blackpool to find work. Once there, she very nearly collided with a tram, then sang in a Song-pluggers' Parlour and visited the Pleasure Beach. All Blackpool was revealed to a national audience.

The link is tenuous, but it is just possible that this revelation might have been seen and appreciated for the phenomenon it was. In the film Gracie Fields meets the Boss's son (also on holiday in democratic Blackpool). Could this have sparked off Thomas's reference to mill proprietor and millhand meeting 'with complete democratic equality'?

All this is conjecture. The mid-thirties were becoming (but were not yet positively) aware of the Deep North. It was still a curiosity which Mass Observation was beginning to investigate and George Orwell to write about. In retrospect both attempts were condescending and ham-fisted, and the Grierson documentary film makers were just getting into their stride.

But two things are certain about the heyday year of 1936. Professor Edrington-Green enjoyed himself hugely on the Pleasure Beach and Leonard Thompson got valuable publicity for it just in time for the autumn Illuminations.

'Illuminations' of a different sort were on show in London at exactly the same time. The latest scientific miracle, television, was to be introduced shortly (the world's first high-definition regular service was due to open in November) and a series of programmes was produced to coincide with Radiolympia. At Olympia (and no doubt in Joseph Emberton's Empire Hall there) the screens flickered and Adele Dixon appeared to sing the specially composed song to celebrate the opening. It began:

A mighty maze of mystic magic rays
Is all about us in The Blue

and ended (again without any reference to the major scientific development it was):

Conjured up in Sound and Sight
By the magic of the Light
That brings television to you.

And in the middle was the couplet:

The world is at your door—
It's out there, just for you to view

'The world out there' included televising Blackpool Illuminations, but not for twenty years.

20 An Hotel's Story

Aspirations and frustrations. Vita-glass, Vi-springs and finest cuisine

Hotels have often been used as the setting for a story, play or film but few hotels, apart from a handful of grand international ones can tell their own story. By a fortunate accident (the preservation of a file of business and personal correspondence, estimates and invoices and suchlike) the story of one of the hotels on the New South Promenade can be told.

The Headlands Hotel stands at the southern end of Bourne Crescent, the first section of the New South Promenade to be developed. The site was acquired in 1930 and the choice was deliberate—facing west and south (towards the sun and overlooking the proposed green area of Harrowside). The choice did not meet with the wholehearted approval of the redoubtable Maud Bourne, who was the originator of and moving spirit behind the development. She saw the crescent developing from the northern end and the site for the Headlands was remote with a vast area of undeveloped ground in between.

The purchasers, however, insisted that this was the site they wanted, not one facing north and west as she proposed. Here again a personality is paramount—a name (that of a man, later of a family), weaving itself tightly into the fabric of a story.

C. F. Rickards was not a Blackpool native; nor was he a hotelier. At the time he was a successful Manchester gold and diamond merchant living in Colwyn Bay and commuting (as so many businessmen did) from North Wales to the city daily. But as soon as the decision had been made he and his young family uprooted themselves and moved into the Colwyn Hotel, just a little way along the crescent, to superintend the erection of their own hotel.

The architect for the Bourne Crescent area was a local one—Halstead Best (later to collaborate with Joseph Emberton on the

Casino building at the Pleasure Beach) and the hotel opened in July 1931. With twenty bedrooms it was a modest affair but by 1933 it had been extended to thirty-three by the addition of a section on the southern (Harrowside) face. By 1936 there were plans for an additional storey, bringing it up to fifty rooms. In a letter to the Corporation Rickards pointed out that when his scheme was finished he would have 'not much short of £20,000' involved—a substantial sum for these Depression years.

By 1936 Bourne Crescent was finished, two hotels had been added overlooking Harrowside, further hotels were being erected north of the crescent (between it and the Pleasure Beach) and much of the northern end of Clifton Drive had been built.

Harrowside is the subject of Rickards' letter to the Council, but in pressing his complaints about the Council's failure to develop the green area, Rickards has left a graphic picture of the aspirations and frustrations of the hoteliers of the time.

> It was confidently hoped by people that, after the enthusiastic approval shown for this land to be kept as open space, the Council would have lost no time in formulating a scheme which would prove an agreeable amenity to the town and an attraction to those who desired to spend their leisure time on the South Shore.
>
> Instead . . . the land lies in its stark and barren unattractiveness and thousands of visitors passing through cast an enquiring eye on this site and no doubt wonder what future is in store for it.
>
> To these thousands it may only be of passing or slight interest; but to the several scores of hotel keepers who have had the courage to put up some hundred of thousands of pounds of capital in the erecting and equipping of hotels on the South Promenade, the matter is of vital importance.

This is straightforward, no-nonsense stuff, coming directly to the point—the money. Rickards may only have been a Blackpool resident for some five years but he had learned what made the town tick—and the Councillors sit up!

The open green space at Harrowside was controversial. The street-plan for the New South Promenade development envisaged two crescents fronting on to the broad promenade separated by an open 'green' reaching back as far as the railway line. Hotels (the two built next to the Headlands) looked across the green from north and south and even the abutments of the railway bridge received an architectural treatment—altogether an accomplished unified plan.

At some stage during the development it was proposed that a huge hotel should be built on the open area and this move was strenuously opposed by the local hoteliers with Rickards prominent in the arguments. He referred to it as 'a haven of green peace' which may have been overstating the issue but was true in essence; Harrowside was (and still is) the only major break in the building line along the Promenade between the Gynn and Squires Gate. It also remains as a modestly shining example of what can be done within the framework of a 'commercial' development.

Rickards' letter continues:

> Four and a half years ago I had erected on what was a very derelict site the above hotel . . . I was, so to speak, a pioneer and took a risk that no-one else, at the time, seemed willing to take. The promenade was completed and there was a certain wide spaciousness about the locality which was attractive, but it needed plenty of courage in face of all sorts of adverse opinion, but I felt, at the time, that I had a go-ahead Corporation behind me and whatever efforts I was likely to put forward, the Council would not be lacking in their efforts also.
>
> You will perhaps remember that The Headlands stood alone for some considerable time and then the locality began to spring forward with tremendous rapidity. My venture at this corner developed the New South Promenade, so far as the building of hotels is concerned, at least five years before its time until now it is a moot point as to whether the development has not been too rapid.

So far, the letter has been concerned with an observation of the situation, an accurate record of the development of the site alongside the new Promenade. We are, after all, talking about a development sanctioned twenty years before and opened ten years before. Undoubtedly, the particular combination of personalities had produced the group of modestly luxurious hotels at a time when Blackpool's image was being firmly set by the Rector of Stiffkey and the 'Kiss me quick' (more likely 'Kiss me kwik'!) hats. They had also been more-than-modestly successful—witness the extensions to the Headlands and the other hotels going up nearby.

Confining his observations to the immediate area (and studiously avoiding reference to the controversy over Harrowside) Rickards goes on to express concern, then issue a veiled—but positive threat.

> During the whole of this time there has been no single improvement . . .
> and I think it is an alarming and serious state of affairs and unless
> something is done to remedy this defect, many of the hotel keepers will
> be forced to dispose of their interests in their businesses or resort to
> other desperate means of keeping going . . .
> I cannot help thinking that the utmost expedition is necessary to
> make the Harrowside plot as attractive as possible . . .
> It is of paramount importance to me and to others that the South Side
> be made much more attractive and I believe that, if the Council can be
> persauded to take a broad view . . . they will be rewarded by a splendid
> response from visitors . . . and they will earn the hearty co-operation of
> the whole of the hotel keepers who only want a fair deal for them to put
> forth their best efforts.

This letter, preserved almost by accident, paints a vivid picture
of both the man and the town. It was, after all, the diamond jubilee
of the incorporation as a Borough, but one senses a frustration with
the ordering of things. The sons of the founding fathers were still
prominent—maybe dominant in the running of the town. Did
Rickards, as a newcomer, feel left out of things? Quality he certainly
had, and business expertise—he was still commuting daily and
actively involved with his business interests in Manchester. It is not
unreasonable to think of him labelled as an 'outsider', a bit too 'cut-
glass' for Blackpool.

It is equally reasonable to see the lack of development at
Harrowside as deliberate—a retaliation for Rickards' spirited
defence of the 'haven of green peace'. Times were changing and it
was all a far cry from the days when Lindsay Parkinson could buy
the Blackpool & Fleetwood Tramroad and present the Council with
a casual fait accompli and an invitation to buy at what he'd paid for
it.

The letter—the very phrasing of it—reveals a colourful character. C. F. Rickards was, above all else, an individual. He could
address a Council Chairman formally: 'the utmost expedition is
necessary to make the Harrowside plot attractive', or at a firmly
personal level: 'the hotel keepers (not, note 'hoteliers') only want a
fair deal'.

The *Daily Express* no less, found how much of an individual

Rickards could be. They had published an article about Blackpool which included a portrait of the Headlands and, significantly, Mrs Rickards, who was responsible for the day-to-day running of the hotel. The article made her out to be some typical Blackpool Landlady—'all bosom and bark'—in line with the boozy Golden Mile image but not with Rickards' view of his spouse.

Mass circulation, Beaverbrook or no, Rickards went for the editor (via his solicitor), threatening him with dire consequences. Reading the correspondence one feels the editor was lucky to escape with his life, never mind his position as Northern Editor! The Headlands, after all, advertised in the *Manchester Guardian*. In common with *The Times*, the *Manchester Guardian*'s front page consisted of column after column of tightly-knit adverts. Rickards' stands out by its personal (yet somehow 'period') style:

> THE GENTLE ART OF WHEEDLING
> After their cruise last summer, Mother
> persuaded Dad that he couldn't possibly go
> back and bury himself in that stuffy old
> office for three months without a single break
> and that he must take her for a week to
>
> THE HEADLANDS
>
> South Promenade, Blackpool
>
> They certainly came back full of that joie-de-
> vivre that speaks perfect health; their second
> visit is planned for early September.
>
> Fifty bedrooms with H&C Water. Vi-spring beds
> Sea Water baths, finest cuisine. Lift.
> Inclusive Terms from 12/6d a Day. Book now
>   Garage
> FULLY APPOINTED AA AND RAC.

The 1930s is written into every line, the superior status of the hotel framing the whole. Handbasins were not universal, even in the better hotels. The lift was a luxury. The garage marked the hotel out as a modern one, the use of the words 'cuisine' and 'joie-de-vivre' as a better-than average one. Beds and food have always been basic essentials in hotel-keeping and here visitors are in no doubt that the beds will not be made up from the old flock mattresses.

'Dad', though, works in an office, not in the weaving shed and he and Mother have been on a cruise. They are in a position to take three holidays a year (and likely, also, to need that garage). The tariff is steep, considering the average wages were around £2 10s a week. Three years later Rickards was offering a prospective long-term guest an out-of-season price of 3 guineas a week for a back room or 4 guineas for one facing the sea.

By 1939, the Headlands had added a sun lounge (Vita-glass of course), the first hotel on Bourne Crescent to add one. Significantly, perhaps, Halstead Best have given way to Derham, MacKeith & Partners, who have a spidery Gill-Sans lettering to their business notepaper and Rickards is complaining, somewhat petulantly, about the delays in finishing the work and the quality of some of the items involved. Soon, however, he was to be involved in far weightier matters—literally.

The outbreak of war in September 1939 brought immediate problems. The West Coast was considered safe and Blackpool was to be left to continue as a holiday resort—but with reservations. Civil servants were to be billeted in some of the hotels. Rickards reacted immediately—but not helpfully. On 6 October, barely a month after the outbreak of the war he was writing to his MP:

> . . . I do hope something will be done to leave me undisturbed at The Headlands where I am carrying on such a successful business. It does seem fatal to destroy a successful business when there are so many around who are unfortunately only making their expenses, who can be utilised for billetting Government Officials.

Barely had he tackled this problem than he was faced with another—in the shape of the Local Fuel Overseer, who was responsible for the allocation of coal for heating the hotel. Politely, but firmly, he writes:

> I beg to make application for a larger supply of fuel as I find the deduction of 25% from my last year's consumption of about 70 tons will bear very hardly on the permanent residents of the hotel and as some of these are in the region of 80 years of age I feel that the application I am making will commend itself to your consideration. My ordinary allowance for the four quarters from September 30th 1938 were as follows:

1st Quarter   11 tons 15 cwts.
2nd Quarter   23 tons 17 cwts.
3rd Quarter   20 tons 7 cwts.
4th Quarter   14 tons 15 cwts.

If you can possibly allow me to receive up to this amount I should be most extremely obliged.

His application was successful (the 'most extremely obliged' may have done the trick). In view of the hard winter of 1939–40 it was fortuitous!

During the protracted correspondence with the Government authorities during the early days of the war Rickards found cause to call in a higher authority—the Right Honourable David Lloyd George himself, no less. A persuasive paragraph catches the eye:

I have no actual call upon yourself only that I am of Welsh descent and have been an admirer of yours since the old Birmingham Town Hall days. I am a Manchester man as you yourself are and I feel the contents of this letter which are self-explanatory would appeal to your sense of justice and fairness and that you might be able to do something in the matter.

Welsh, a Manchester man and an admirer since the earlier heady days? That plus the appeal to an elder statesman's sense of justice and fairness? The combination is irresistible!

C. F. Rickards was a man of his time—absolutely self-assured, not suffering fools gladly, prepared to take on the Chairman of the Committee for Town Improvements, the *Daily Express* or the whole of the government single-handed; yet there is not one milligram of malice in his make-up. He strides determinedly through the 1930s, seeing his hotel built on its isolated site, expand, add first thirteen then a further seventeen rooms, develop and mature. The file lights up what would otherwise be indifferent years and highlights the fashions and preoccupations of the age.

Cheek-by-jowl with the letters to the Council, Lloyd George, the Chairman of the Automobile Association (asking for a progress report on the installation of the approval sign), the Local Fuel Overseer and the rest are other snippets of memorabilia. There is a subscription to a local golf club—14gns. He writes approvingly of the quality of a brand of frozen peas, less approvingly of the quality of some items supplied for the sun lounge. An estate agent writes to point out that the small hotel next door may shortly be on the market and draws Mr Rickards' attention to its excellent appointments. Presumably failing to get a reply he writes again; both letters are preserved. Near the end of the file is a brochure for a holiday arranged for Mr Rickards in Biarritz. The year is 1939.

The solarium (then referred to as 'sun shelter and lounge') at Harrowside was barely completed when the War broke out and the green itself was not developed until after the war. Rickards had pointed out that:

> There is a great dearth of tennis courts, bowling greens and other such attractions for the young people who have to go great distances to enjoy the games they are keen on.

Bowling greens and tennis courts there are not, but there is a putting green and Harrowside is still a 'haven of green peace' and a pleasant place to relax on a sunny afternoon. There is still a 'certain wide spaciousness about the locality' and it is still attractive. There is still, for that matter, a Rickards in charge of the Headlands.

21 Blackpool Illuminations

The Greatest Free Show on Earth—worth millions, and an earl to cheer as well

At the time of year when other British resorts are putting up the shutters and preparing for the winter quiet, Blackpool takes a deep breath, offers up a quick prayer for fair weather and light winds, switches on its Illuminations and launches itself into the most hectic weeks of its long season.

The statistics are formidable. The Illuminations are continuous over the 6 miles from Starr Gate to Little Bispham and use 375,000 lamps. Currently it costs Blackpool over three quarters of a million pounds to stage the autumn show—80 per cent from the Corporation and the rest from the local business community. An individual set-piece can take three years to develop from first sketch to glittering final product and employ 100 workmen in its manufacture. One monster 60ft tableau built for the 1981 Illuminations cost £15,000 and absorbed 125,000 man-hours.

The visitors pour in in their millions; 3 million of them stay in the resort for four days or more. The Pleasure Beach estimates it gets 30 per cent of its income from the whole season during the fifty-nine days of the Illuminations. The 2,000 people working there and the 12,000 employed in the tourist business in Blackpool work two months more a year than they would otherwise. All this takes place during September and October with late summer sliding into a windy winter; gale damage must be repaired within twenty-four hours and twenty men are on duty at all times to carry out this essential work.

Every evening motor coaches leave the towns of the North for an excursion to 'the Lights'—a traditional autumn treat. Nowadays with the motorways bringing half the population of Britain within two hours of Blackpool the evening trip is possible from much further away. Excursion trains are run from as far away as London and Scotland. The traffic on the Promenade runs one-way, south to north, twin lines of snail-paced traffic all the way from Starr Gate to Little Bispham. The effects of the traffic are felt all over the Fylde—and the glow in the sky can be seen from the Isle of Man 60 miles away across the sea.

The lights are not simply strung—they are massed, looped, garlanded along and across the full width of the Promenade. Vividly coloured butterflies (or cartoon animals or bouquets of multi-coloured flowers or anything else that has taken the designer's fancy) glitter on the lampposts, above the centre of the road, on arches built across the road—even atop the public lavatories. The Tower is outlined in lights zipping up one side and down the other, every window of the town hall is framed with individual lamps.

North of Uncle Tom's Cabin the extravagant festoons of light give way to an even more spectacular display—elaborate tableaux set on the greens between the tramroad and the sea, their backs to the dark night sky, their faces towards the thousands in their cars, on coaches and trams. Circus clowns tumble, footballers kick flickering balls across a diamond-studded field, Disneyesque figures in moulded glass-fibre and lit from inside wave their arms at the crowds and nod their heads, peacocks flare their multi-coloured tails. In 1981, Royal Wedding year, Charles and Diana smiled graciously, then flickered away to reveal a huge union jack of many hundreds of red-white-blue lamps. Few of the spectators realised that the three-year development process had been cut to the handful of months between the announcement and the opening of the Illuminations.

The trams join in with a string of mobile set-pieces. The much-loved Venetian gondola of pre-war days has given way to *HMS Blackpool*, a rocketship *Tramnik One*—a solid mass of glittering lamps. A Mississippi steamboat sails along, waves rippling away from its bow, a Western Train—locomotive and carriage, complete with cowcatcher, bell and, at one time, real non-functional smoke makes its glittering way along between the service cars.

All this, a glittering show which is mesmeric and almost overpowering is a home-grown effort, entirely the product of the Blackpool mind and Blackpool's hands. It expresses the spirit of the place, totally and unequivocally, a solid 6 miles of open-handed, warm-hearted fun and good humour there for everyone to enjoy. They call it 'the Greatest Free Show on Earth' and it is worth £75 million to the resort every year!

Many other resorts have their illuminations—Morecambe's are preferred by some where the showpieces are set in the sea–front Happy Mount Park. Douglas has them all summer and every sea-side holiday town puts on some sort of show. They cannot compare and if wise they will not compete. A Blackpool landlady took one look at Southend's considerable effort and remarked 'Huh! Nobbut a string o'beads!'.

In a sense, the trams began it all in Blackpool, when five illuminated conduit cars amazed the holidaymakers of 1897. They were partly to celebrate the Diamond Jubilee and partly to celebrate the decision to end the much-disliked system and go over to trolley power collection. Then, inspired by a local worthy who had visited Berlin and seen the illuminations staged to celebrate the Kaiser's birthday, Blackpool erected decorative lighting to coincide with the opening of the new stretch of promenade round the Metropole Hotel by HRH Princess Louise in May 1912. At the suggestion of a local newspaper the lights were switched on again in September; the result was that Blackpool had its best season ever. The show was revived in 1913 and again in 1914, a month after the outbreak of war. This time one local newspaper was not so kind. 'It is time', it said, 'to ring down the curtain on this sorry spectacle.'

A lengthy fuel crisis after the War prevented the resumption of the Illuminations, so in 1923 Blackpool staged a massive June Carnival. Not only was it inspired by the carnivals in Nice but workmen were brought in from the South of France to manufacture the oversized moulded heads for the procession figures. Somewhat incongruously, the workmen were housed in a building which was part of the tram depot; equally incongruously, the workshop was always known as 'the Carnival Shop' even when returned to the Transport Department.

The Carnival of 1923 was a resounding success ('an almost embarrassing success' it was said) and was repeated the following year. 1924 was a disaster; ruined by drunkenness and hooliganism (forty years before the Mods and Rockers at Margate—Blackpool scored another 'first'!). The Carnival was dropped and the Illuminations resumed for twenty-nine days in 1925.

The General Strike of May 1926 ruined the early part of the holiday season and the Illuminations were suspended after three days when the Council was warned it was contravening the fuel regulations in force as a result of the miners' continuing strike. All the same, the Lights were there to celebrate, however briefly, the town's golden jubilee and the opening of the New South Promenade the following Saturday.

From 1927 onwards, the Lights continued annually until 1939. There were some regular features. An illuminated tram—an ordinary double-decker outlined in lamps and with the slogans 'Welcome to our visitors' 'Health and Pleasure' and the town's motto, the single defiant word 'Progress'—which had been a feature since the inception in 1912, was joined by a graceful Venetian gondola, albeit with its cabin placed amidships to disguise the trolley pole. The season was extended, the extravaganza grew; 10,000 people goggled at the Rector of Stiffkey in a single day, 1,250 special excursion trains pulled in at the Blackpool stations for the Lights.

The Illuminations were restored after World War II in 1949, lighting up—and lightening—the grey post-war austerity years. The Lights went on television, with their own television tramcar, a decided novelty in the early 1950s. There is a story that Leonard Thompson had had a disagreement with the BBC regarding televising some of the features on the Pleasure Beach. As the mobile cameras approached the glittering spectacle of the Pleasure Beach dressed overall for the Illuminations every light went out—on Thompson's orders. If the story isn't true, it *ought* to be. The British Broadcasting Corporation might be a Power in the Land, but this was Blackpool—and Blackpool would cut anybody down to size if they got above themselves!

Commercial Television arrived and ABC Television (the ill-fated 'Northern Weekend' company which disappeared in an early reshuffle of franchises) sponsored the Western Train tram feature. Then came 625-lines and colour and at last the country saw an approximation to the true glory of Blackpool in the autumn. The Illuminations had cost something of the order of £50,000 to stage in 1949; now it was well over ten times that amount.

A celebrity is invited to throw the switch to light up the town each year and the list of names through the years is almost a catalogue of changing fashions in that strange phenomenon, celebrity. There was George Formby, the footballer Stanley Matthews, more recently Doctor Who, the Muppets, the Grand National Winner Red Rum, then Violet Carson, a local resident, and looking, off-duty, totally unlike her Ena Sharples of 'Coronation Street' image.

There was the famous occasion in 1959 (and recorded on film for posterity) when Jayne Mansfield, Hollywood sex symbol *par excellence* and a classic example of the transient quality of fame mounted the dais outside the town hall to perform the opening ceremony. The Mayor (perhaps put slightly off his stroke by the lady's oddly pneumatic quality) referred to her repeatedly as 'Jean'. The crowd roared and Miss Mansfield kept on smiling bravely. Ad-libbing desperately the Mayor said, 'Well, you don't want to listen to me . . .'—and the crowd roared in agreement!

Clearly, Blackpool could not hope to attract Their Royal Highnesses in their wedding year but they secured the services of the Earl and Countess Spencer of Althorp, who were a resounding success, particularly with the vast crowd jammed into Talbot Square. Any fears that the Earl might not quite fit in with the breezy, happy-go-lucky atmosphere of Blackpool were dispelled immediately. The Earl and Countess, he announced, had spent holidays in Blackpool themselves.

The crowd cheered. Earl he might be, Barbara Cartland's daughter she might be. His parents-in-law they might be, but Earl and Countess were just like Them! Earl Spencer beamed. He insisted that 'if anyone wants a good holiday, come to Blackpool!'. The crowd cheered again. 'It doesn't matter', said the Earl, 'if they live in Sweden, Switzerland or the Outer Hebrides, they'll never get a better holiday!'

The crowd loved that, and roared its approval. 'And', went on Earl Spencer. 'It's got the best funfair in Europe!'. The roar from the crowd almost blew the thousands of lamps in Talbot Square right out of their sockets! 'Blackpool', he concluded, 'is looking the Recession *straight in the eye!*' They cheered him, sang 'Land of Hope and Glory' for him and took him to their hearts. 'Bring yer sister-in-law next time', bellowed a man in the crowd. And it all went out on television, just as the Wedding had gone out two months before!

Later in the same programme a discussion was staged between the indefatigable Brian Redhead, Blackpool's Director of Tourism and Attractions and Geoffrey Thompson, Leonard's son and the present administrator of the Pleasure Beach. The setting *was* the glittering dazzling Pleasure Beach (the BBC had learned its lesson!). Asked why the Illuminations were so overwhelmingly popular the Director of Tourism said simply (but very firmly), 'It's the atmosphere—a carnival feeling.' As if on cue Geoffrey Thompson added, '*We* have a Notting Hill Carnival *every* day!'

To anyone steeped in the tradition that the British are reserved and take their pleasures sadly Blackpool at any time comes as something of a shock. To see it during the Illuminations totally demolishes, disorientates, and then rebuilds such a person in minutes. It quickens the pulse, brightens the eye and speeds the step. It refreshes and rejuvenates before the long dark winter. It is unforgettable and irresistible. A world-weary Londoner, used to the West End lights, the spectacle of New York by night, the colourful pleasures of San Francisco suddenly stopped, rooted to the spot. 'Why can't everywhere', he demanded, 'be like this *all the time?*' And he hadn't yet seen the Pleasure Beach!

22 Morecambe

By Little North Western to Yorkshire-by-the-Sea, where beauty surrounds, health abounds and Black Dyke plays in the arena

The peninsula between the Lune and Morecambe Bay contains all the threads which, woven together produce the fabric which is the heritage of the Lancashire Coast. Warp and weft threads are the same—old villages submerged in a modern seaside resort, fishing and transport, the changeling sea, the industrial North clanking away in the background.

Once again, the combination of landscape, history and people produces a fabric which is subtly different, and in the case of the peninsula one which is richly compact. The landscape is markedly different. The Cumbrian mountains are the northern horizon; they and the Pennines fold round the promontory and shelter it, giving the towns and villages a softer outline than the more exposed towns of the Fylde coast. There is a sense of distance and scale that is lacking in, for instance, Southport. Yet the scale is smaller, the style more workaday. Morecambe and Heysham is a series of bays set round a convex curve, each hidden from the rest and Heysham, at least, gives some modest cliffs and rocky coves. Behind, the estuarial marsh stretches away to the Lune.

Morecambe's old villages are virtually obliterated now, even though Poulton-le-Sands (Morecambe's historical name) was a sizeable settlement of 1,500 people when Blackpool was a third the size. But Heysham remains, ravaged by commercialism in some eyes, retaining the look of a small village. Inevitably it is compared to Clovelly in Devon (but so is every village which has a street winding downhill whether or not it ends at the sea!). Morecambe itself is said to be 'architecturally undistinguished', but the occasional fine terrace of Victorian hotels stands out as do the Art Deco Midland Hotel, the outstanding modern Leisure Park and a group of hotels at the eastern end of the Promenade (which, on examination, turn out to be carbon copies of those on the New South Promenade at Blackpool). The local stone is greyer, 'cooler' than the rich Rossendale sandstone of St Annes and the local style is less exuberant. Morecambe is not so consciously tree-girt as Southport or St Annes, yet not so lacking as Blackpool, and it has hills, rising terraces and curving streets which break the often monotonous lines of the usual sea-front.

Historically, time is 'stretched'. Lancaster, with all that that implies, is close by (Morecambe is now, in fact, part of the City of Lancaster) and history is a saleable commodity. Heysham has legends of St Patrick, Viking graves and a church on Saxon foundations. Heysham also has a port, sixty years younger than Fleetwood and swapping punches with it for most of its lifetime. It also has a nuclear power station, and this, according to some, could be Morecambe's latest historical relic. Stand by the Viking graves on Heysham head and it is possible to see them all—and the timeless mountains of the Lake District.

The third ingredient, people, are, again, subtly different. Morecambe was inevitably compared with Blackpool, yet it lacked its individual entrepreneurs; and here there was no great ideal as expounded by Hesketh Fleetwood. Morecambe is the product of careful local people working on a conceivable scale, producing a town that was small and easily managed, yet varied and accomplished. Also, it was just that bit further away from the industrial belts, less accessible to the would-be seaside resident. All the same, it was the nearest easily accessible bit of coastal air and scenery to the merchants of Bradford and Leeds and a surprisingly large number set up home there and endured a two-hour commuter journey morning and night.

The railway companies could be counted as 'people'; they stamped their personality on Poulton-le-Sands and made it Morecambe. The silting of the Lune had for many years inhibited the progress of Lancaster as a port (and at the time of the construction of the Lancaster Canal there had been a proposal to make a cut from it to the open sea at Poulton-le-Sands) and in 1846 the 'Little North Western' Railway proposed an extension from

Lancaster to a 'port' on the shores of Morecambe Bay. The Morecambe Harbour and Railway Act received Parliamentary sanction that year—the 'Morecambe' referring to the Bay rather than any village on it.

Seen as an outlet for the traffic to Ireland and Scotland, the railway line was extended on to a massive stone pier jutting out from the headland just south of the village of Poulton-le-Sands and the first station was on the jetty; by 1850 the port of 'Morecambe' was handling twice the tonnage of Glasson, the port built to link the Lancaster Canal to the sea.

The spur to development provided by the railway and port was short-lived; by the mid 1860s, the Midland Railway concluded a deal with the newly-opened Furness Railway round the north side of the bay to re-route its Irish traffic to Roa Island in the Piel channel near Barrow-in-Furness. Later still, the company switched to Barrow itself, then finally to its new harbour at Heysham. Morecambe remained a port, but not the major outlet envisaged when the stone pier was built.

But the impetus provided by the coming of the railway lasted long enough to get the new resort off the ground. The well-to-do of Lancashire and Yorkshire (particularly Yorkshire) found a convenient watering place on the shores of an attractive bay and by 1881 the 'Topography and Directory of Lancaster and 16 miles round' was able to report:

> Poulton-le-Sands, now better known as Morecambe, is a clean, healthy and popular watering place . . . and now contains several streets and handsome terraces etc., with numerous well-appointed shops, hotels, inns and lodging houses for the reception and accommodation of visitors and tourists, for whose use there is a large supply of vehicles and pleasure boats. The crescent opposite the bay is a fine range of buildings and there are four first class hotels, several bazaars, and the Morecambe baths, Palace and Aquarium, a place much resorted to for recreation and amusement and in which are two public salt baths for gentlemen and one for ladies, besides twenty-four private and two medicated baths.

But another observer wrote of the growing town: 'a combination of narrow streets, very dull or very shoppy, and a staring Promenade with "Amusements" written loud and large all over it.

There is a tiresome multitude of "souvenirs" for sale and the whole place speaks of "crowd".'

He could equally well have been writing of that other, larger resort 15 miles away on the Fylde Coast. The comparisons with Blackpool were insidious as well as inevitable and the rivalry predictable and unwelcome from Morecambe's point of view. Blackpool had three piers, Morecambe two. Both had their Winter Gardens—Morecambe's an ornate terra-cotta building with a splendid theatre. For Blackpool's Grand Theatre, read Morecambe's Royalty, both designed by Frank Matcham. Morecambe never emulated Blackpool's splendid line of Victorian hotels on the North Promenade but it had some neat developments along its West End promenade.

And Morecambe had its Tower. In fact, in its time it had two! One was a curious revolving device on a site near Promenade Station and the other, had it ever been finished, would have incorporated features even Blackpool had not thought of. It was to be of the order of 250ft high, and was to have a spiral road round the outside which, the prospectus said 'will gradually ascend by easy gradients from the ground to this platform [the top presumably] which may also be reached by an electric tramway or hydraulic lifts. The greater portion of the first circuit will represent an oriental thoroughfare or market place.'

The oriental theme was incorporated in the design of the building at the foot of the tower which contained a pavilion capable of seating 5,000 people. The prospectus of the Morecambe Tower Company was issued in 1898 and the pavilion and part of the skeleton of the tower were completed before the depression after the Boer War brought a halt. The tower was never completed and during World War I the whole structure was demolished and the steel used for munitions. The pavilion remained, and in the golden days of the 1930s was a primary entertainment rendezvous. It closed under the name of the Gaumont—an outlet for the Rank Organisation—in 1959 and was subsequently demolished. A block of luxury flats was intended for the site but in the event a structure of curiously 'bunker-like' appearance was built and the Tower (then Gaumont) received a new lease of life as a Granada Bingo hall.

Morecambe started late and developed fast, and developed in a strangely haphazard way. The sea-trade went and in its place came a ship-breakers' yard—in the dead centre of a bustling holiday resort; visitors to the elegant Midland hotel must have been somewhat surprised to see famous transatlantic liners like the *Majestic* being dismembered before their eyes! Horse trams continued to run until 1926 (and the decision to scrap them was by no means unanimous even then) yet electric trains had run between Lancaster and Morecambe from the early date of 1908. The line, with its overhead collection of current and peculiarly graceful trains was an experiment in electric traction by the Midland Railway, its only venture into this kind of transport.

The line ran from the Midland Company's Green Ayre station at Lancaster virtually in a straight line to Morecambe, and when the new road to the resort from the north side of Skerton bridge was built alongside it gave this section of the line the appearance of an interurban tramway. The line continued from Morecambe to the new harbour at Heysham—a gigantic venture designed to give the railway a deep-water port unaffected by the vagaries of the tide and an outlet to rival Holyhead and Liverpool.

The London & North Western Railway also ran to Morecambe, its line branching off from the main London–Glasgow line and curving round to its own station at, appropriately, Euston Road terminus. The Midland, however, reigned supreme, whisking passengers from Yorkshire up its own main line to Settle then across to the Lune valley, Lancaster (the very heart of the Red Rose County) and on to its own bit of Yorkshire-by-the-Sea. It proclaimed its supremacy at Promenade Station, a splendid Tudoresque building in the best 'quality' Midland Railway style with the sea only yards away. By contrast, the LNWR, for all its title 'the Premier Line' crept in to a modest building well away from the Promenade.

Morecambe became a Borough in 1902 but did not appoint a full-time Town Clerk until 1920, and did not have a purpose-built town hall until 1932 (by which time it had absorbed Heysham). But when it finally built a town hall it built a classic—splendidly 'municipal neo-georgian' and set firmly on the sea-front, or rather, nearly on the sea-front; immediately before its construction it was found that the ground was unstable and the building was set back a little from its original line.

The villages, Torrisholme, Bare and Heysham remained identifiable for a time, but Torrisholme and Bare virtually disappeared in the swell of development between the wars. As at Blackpool, the Promenade was extended and the development appeared along it, then behind it. The Sandylands Promenade crept along towards Heysham, the Central Promenade was extended beyond the Tower then round the curve of the bay towards Hest Bank. On this latter section a group of hotels were built in identical style to those on the New South Promenade and the same remarkable woman, Maud Bourne, was responsible.

Again, the names are evocative—'Mayfair', 'Strathmore', 'St Winifred's' and—significantly and appropriately 'Broadway'. This was Mrs Bourne's masterpiece. The hotels, even those in Blackpool, were originally three storeys high. The Broadway is five and is set on a prominent corner site and has a totally unnecessary but architecturally fitting semi-circular colonnaded entrance porch. And unlike its Blackpool contemporaries, the Broadway remains in its original style, right down to 'sunburst' leaded lights in the upper part of the window frames. It is a 'grand' hotel (in every sense but the forbidding) and, as an indication of its (and its originator's) position in the town its foundation stone was laid by the Mayor. Its date is important—1936; the end of a line which began with Bourne Crescent at Blackpool only six years before.

The holidaymaker of the mid-1930s, in a country just beginning to lift itself off the ground after the Great Depression, looked on his visit to the seaside as the big experience of the year. The Northerner, particularly, had one week's holiday only, fixed for his town's annual Wakes Week. Since he worked a five-and-a-half-day week the weekend trip was impossible and only a minority would break with the responsibilities of Sunday to head for the sea. Everything was, by necessity, concentrated into that one glorious summer week.

Reservations for accommodation had been made months before—often the same boarding house year after year or one personally recommended by friends. Requirements were quite specific and the advertisements of the time give an idea of the priorities. There is a strong emphasis on good cooking, cleanliness and 'homeliness'. The smaller establishments often placed the name of the proprietress (and it is almost always a proprietress) above the name of the house. The northern 'clan' system was still strong and if you knew a Mrs Duckworth in Bolton or Baildon her counterpart in Blackpool or Morecambe was likely to prove more satisfactory than a Mrs McIntosh or O'Grady—she had, after all, married into a good solid northern family.

The apartments system was popular. The visitor bought his own food and the landlady cooked it for him. He provided his own accompaniments, even down to butter and sugar and the landlady provided a space in the dining room sideboard for them. The 'extra for use of cruet, 1/–' tradition comes from these days. For the food-fad it was an ideal system, but it must have been a nightmare for the landlady with say eight or nine different meat dishes to cook, and always the suspicion that she had extracted a spoonful or two for her own family. 'Apartments' gave thousands of families holidays at minimum cost—say 3s 6d per bed (and very often 'bed' appears in the adverts). Once the bed cost was paid the rest was optional; the visitor ate what he could afford to buy.

The Morecambe Guide for 1935 indicates the way standards were changing. Mrs L. Hargreaves at 'Ivy House' offers both apartments and board residence and points out that there is electric light in all rooms (by no means universal, even in 1935). There is also a garage 'near'. Board is optional so far as Mrs Kershaw (a definitive northern surname) at 'Donendale' in Sefton Road is concerned, and she offers 'public' and 'private' apartments (presumably the luxury of a private dining room). Mrs Allan of Alma House, Clarendon Road has 'homely apartments', beds at 3s 6d and 4s and offers full board at 7s 6d. She stresses her separate tables (usual but not universal) and her 'fires if cold or wet'. 'Electric light throughout' appears often, 'piano' frequently, 'wireless' occasionally and 'indoor sanitation' in a number of cases.

The Wateredge, a substantial hotel on the Sandylands Promenade announces that it has 'recently been enlarged and Hot and Cold Water laid to all Bedrooms'; some establishments stress hot and cold *running* water (so one assumes that the jug and bowl was still found in some places). Few advertise 'interior spring' mattresses (so many, presumably, still used the flock mattresses), fewer still central heating, although many of the larger establishments offer gas fires in most rooms. The larger boarding houses and hotels have lounges, smoking and writing rooms, the smaller ones hardly ever. Guests were required to leave the house immediately after a meal time and not return until the next—'access to rooms all day' was a post-war innovation, as were keys to rooms. Of the hotels advertising in the guide, not one advertises a private bath.

The 1935 *Morecambe and Heysham Holiday Book (Beauty Surrounds, Health Abounds)* has a delightfully informal text—unusual at the time—written by a Mr C. A. MacKay for the Advertising Department of the Corporation. As a foreword, he invites the reader of the guide to 'Come Nor'west this year' and observes:

Every Holiday Book that is issued by any seaside or inland resort is an invitation to spend your leisure days within its delectable boundaries. And just as the towns vary in their amenities and attractions, so do books.

But this book is now in your hands—and we hope that it has conveyed . . . a pleasing first impression of the place and its environs, and caused you to say 'This seems a very cheerful happy, bustling sort of holiday centre: Shall we go to Morecambe?'

We will try very hard not to make this like the old-fashioned guide book, taking you by the hand up one street and down the other, into every nook and cranny, hole and corner. We are looking at things through more modern eyes. Although we admit our town is not yet as up-to-date as we would like it to be, it is coming on apace, and in any case we feel that it can provide you with nearly everything you desire for holiday entertainment in the widest possible sense.

MacKay is refreshingly modest regarding Morecambe's beach: 'while we cannot put forward extravagant claims regarding our sands they have proved amply sufficient for the thousands of children who use them each summer', and he does not gloss over the deficiencies: 'Unfortunately, as I write, the Central Pier is still derelict [it had suffered a disastrous fire the year before] but the new proprietors will speedily be providing up to date amenities to restore it to its former glory.' And he gives credit where it is due. The ship-breakers' yard had finally closed and MacKay remarks:

> People who knew Morecambe will marvel at the metamorphosis. What was the unsightly 'breaking-up-yard' has been transformed into something of utility and beauty. The excellent new bandstand and arena are well illustrated in this book and there is no necessity to enlarge on their popularity.

1935 was Silver Jubilee Year and a full programme of band concerts had been arranged for the new arena. Between July and the end of September twelve bands were scheduled to give concerts, including Fodens, Black Dyke, and Wingates and the regimental bands of the Welch Regiment, the Gordon Highlanders, the Sherwood Foresters, 16th–5th Lancers, RASC, Royal Corps of Signals and King's Own Royal Regiment. MacKay comments:

> I believe, even in 1935, in the days of radio and gramophone and talkie, that everybody still likes 'to stroll along the prom, prom, prom. Where

the brass band plays tiddly-om-pom-pom.' There is something so essentially 'sea-sidey' about the cheerful strains of a good band, and about the appearance of the bandsmen 'in scarlet and in gold' [The bands]. . . play on Sundays in the enclosure at Happy Mount Park, and weekdays in the wonderful new arena at the Harbour Gardens (the finest in Britain).

At this time Morecambe had its own Kursaal, the Holy Well Spa, on the sea-front near the Winter Gardens. The water was not exactly local (it was brought over from the spring on Humphrey Head on the north side of the Bay) but its availability gave Morecambe the edge over its rivals. As MacKay points out:

> Comparable in its proved virtues with the famous waters of Continental and British Spas, it is an additional holiday attribute which, allied to the beneficent effects of glorious sunshine, tonic sea-mountain air and particularly pure, soft, well aerated drinking water, should not be overlooked when all other things may seem equal . . .
>
> It is prescribed for chronic rheumatism, gout, dyspepsia, anaemia, constipation, skin troubles, and as a general tonic. There is no water very near it in composition. Its chief constituents are chlorides of sodium and magnesium, the sulphates of lime, soda and potash and carbonate of lime. The dose is two tumblers full per day—at the Kursaal the price is 3d per glass. It can be obtained in cases of six bottles at 10/6 (12/6 carriage paid).

Close by the Kursaal was the site for the new swimming pool and MacKay launches himself enthusiastically:

> All through the winter, and for some months to come, big gangs of men will be engaged in the construction of a new sea wall, promenade and Britain's most up-to-date luxury open-air swimming bath. Designed to conform with the very latest practice, these will open at the beginning of the 1936 Summer Season.

Elsewhere in the Guide he points out that the new baths will be 'as modern in conception, design and finish as next year's cars or radio.'

Every 1930s holiday guide constantly stresses clean air, sunlight, clean water and their beneficial effects and one tends to forget the contrast there was between the seaside towns and the industrial areas. Many inland towns had barely seen the sun for a century; mills used coal (and there could be a hundred belching mill-chimneys in every town), railways used it and houses were heated by it exclusively. A smoke pall hung over every town from Wigan to Wakefield and the soot literally crunched beneath the feet. Then the damp air (considered important for the spinning and weaving of cotton) added its own hazards in the field of health; Britain had the highest incidence of bronchitis in the world, Lancashire had the highest incidence in Britain. The textile industry added byssinosis—'Weavers' Lung' and the Depression added rickets. Then one can add the contagious diseases brought about by the overcrowded living conditions and the then prevalent outbreaks of whooping cough, scarlet fever and diphtheria!

Probably the biggest environmental change of the past fifty years has been the change in climate in the North of England. Industry going over to electricity (and industry declining) cleared the air considerably; oil and gas-fired central heating cleared it more still. The absence of smoke has given the industrial counties more sunlight, less fog, more night frosts in winter, less oppressive evenings in summer.

The social changes, too, have been remarkable. For all that the textile industry has virtually collapsed and the Lancashire mines at least worked out and recession has hit the North hard, living conditions have improved out of all recognition. The Wakes (Fortnight now) still lingers on but is of less and less importance and the autumn holiday break has become almost as important as the summer vacation. The motorway network is particularly well developed between the industrial towns and the M6, therefore the Lancashire coast is easily accessible. MacKay pointed out in 1935 that Morecambe and Heysham were served by the London Midland & Scottish Railway: 'And we are fortunate in having Britain's Greatest Railway to cater for us'. By the 1960s the slogan was 'M6 for Morecambe'.

Cars in their thousands now bring the visitors to the coast and there is a vast network of coach routes—still a popular way of reaching the resorts; British Rail has, if anything, neglected this side of its business—to its detriment. The means of travel may have changed and the resorts have changed, often out of all recognition, but many a Northerner still insists that a week at Blackpool 'does him good' or an autumn visit to Morecambe 'sets him up for the winter'.

In the golden days of 1935 Morecambe was pointing out that 'Health is the first happiness' and in an eloquent tribute to its own healthiness points out:

> . . . while it is primarily a pleasure resort, catering for . . . young and old in amusement, sport and entertainment — it is also true to say that it has achieved fame because of its health giving attributes. It has become famous all over the North of England as the resort par excellence for those suffering from asthma, bronchitis and other respiratory diseases. Hundreds of people have come to Morecambe to 'die' but they continue to live on. The present Mayor came in 1914 with a 6 months' 'Price' on his Head!

The following year, with the Super Swimming Stadium open, the Mayor (still presumably hale and hearty) laid the foundation stone of the Broadway Hotel and started Morecambe's last great expansion before the war and its consequent changes.

23 An Indian Summer for the Resorts

But the bosom and bark gives way to the sunbed and sauna

If the twenties and thirties were the heyday, then the fifties and early sixties were a kind of Indian summer. Food (and petrol) rationing ended, 'austerity' eased and business boomed; the holiday abroad was still the preserve of the few and package tours were virtually non-existent. Although many Northerners ventured south, the majority stayed loyal to their own resorts.

The traditional 'pattern' still obtained, whole towns (still dominated by the textile industry) moved off to the seaside in a set week. The railways still played an important part in moving the vast crowds—special excursion trains lined up in sidings the night before the start of Wakes Week. On the Saturday morning the town would be as busy as a normal working day, the crowds moving towards the station—a curiously 'slanted' crowd weighed down by heavy suitcases.

The train's rolling stock was often decrepit (pre-1914 Lancashire & Yorkshire Railway and Midland Railway carriages were still running in the 1950s) and the journey tedious. Although the train was scheduled to run non-stop once it had filled up locally it seemed to stop for everything (even, one wit suggested, for the driver to get off and ask the way). A train from the towns of the South Lancashire cotton belt bound for Blackpool could sometimes find itself arriving in Preston by way of Accrington rather than Chorley. (Even today the only passenger trains using the Cliviger Gorge line from Todmorden to Burnley are excursions to the Lancashire Coast from West Yorkshire.)

'Regulation Tickets' (a particularly ruthless term) were necessary for the return journey; they specified which train the traveller would be allowed to return on and the wise queued for these the day they arrived! 'Excursion Platforms' in their dusty splendour existed at all the resorts and British Railways (in the days before it adopted its friendly 'Golden Rail' image) ruled with a rod of iron, steam, smoke and work-worn uncut moquette!

The landlady still ruled, still 'all bosom and bark'. 'Apartments' still existed in a few cases, but the usual arrangement was board residence—breakfast, mid-day dinner, high tea and a light supper—and for a full week. Relatively few establishments (now calling themselves guest houses) accepted mid-week bookings or short stays. The guest houses provided lounges now (often advertised as 'with television') and separate tables and interior spring mattresses were universal, although many houses still thought it wise to list them. 'Access to rooms all day' was a new enough innovation to justify advertising as was 'keys to own room and front door'. (Some landladies, mindful, no doubt of the morals of their guests still locked the front door at eleven and retired for the night. If anyone was still 'out' they were up to no good and could stay out!)

Holiday guides of the period show a transition, though. In Morecambe in 1957 Mrs Grimshaw still chose to put her name above the address of her house in Westminster Road. 'One minute from Sea and Bathing Pool', she gave a choice of bed and breakfast, or tea, bed and breakfast, made concessions on her tariff for OAPs early and late season, had 'spring interiors', a 'garage nearby' 'lounge' and 'H and C all rooms'. The 'Ruskinville Hotel' on the Sandylands Promenade advertised late dinner, central heating, a television lounge and a fully licensed club cocktail bar. At the same time it included the information 'Hot and Cold Running Water in ALL bedrooms, Spring Interior Mattresses on all Beds' and the fact that it was personally supervised by the resident proprietors.

The licensed bar in the hotel was a rarity; the 'Residential' licence was a concession reluctantly granted by the magistrates late on in the post-war period. Even then, few of the 'off Promenade' establishments had such a facility. As late as 1966 the North Bank Hotel in Blackpool (on the Promenade and accommodating 100 guests) thought it judicious to point out that it had a 'Restaurant and Residential Licence'.

A number of the 'traditional values' still applied. The Dunvegan

Private Hotel on the sea front at Cleveleys informs intending visitors in 1963 that it is under personal supervision, has hot and cold water and interior springs in all bedrooms, that there are 'No Petty Restrictions' and, as an additional attraction, it offers 'Excellent Yorkshire Cooking'. At the same time it points out that early booking is advised and there is a 'Four Days Minimum' stay.

The same year in the same resort the 'Sandowne' points out that '80 per cent [of its guests] are return visits or recommendations.' By this time 'apartments' have disappeared, but the first self-catering flats are making their appearance in the Guide Book. A Cleveleys baker and confectioner takes the opportunity to point out that 'When taking your vacation it is essential that you obtain food supplies of the same quality and value with which you are familiar at home. To ensure that your holiday at Cleveleys will be complete, make it your pleasure by shopping at BEAN'S for all your Bread, Pies and Confectionery.'

The resorts relied heavily on their summer shows, and the word 'live' was beginning to creep in in these television days. Morecambe had top West End attractions and the big name artistes at its Winter Gardens and less ambitious shows—*Starlights* at the Marine Theatre on the Central Pier and Hedley Claxton's *Gaytime* (with 'All Star Cast') at the Palace on Sandylands Promenade. But Blackpool reigned supreme with fourteen live shows. Morecambe had to accept defeat and run evening trips from Morecambe to Blackpool!

The mammoth entertainment enterprises were poised to make a move into the resorts in the mid-sixties. They were well aware of the possibilities of a captive audience for twenty or so weeks and poured in their artistes, often, at this time, stars known mainly for their records. Blackpool, which had always kept local control of its main theatre outlets, saw control shift into the hands of London big business and the consequent import of, admittedly, big names but artistes and shows geared for a national, rather than a regional taste. The local-grown talent, used to making a modest living through summer season followed by pantomime, found first the summer, then the winter season taken out of the schedules.

The onslaught of television, rising costs and changing tastes, forced the small town theatres to close and the live theatre contracted dramatically. The big London entrepreneurs found the economics of the seaside resort hard to comprehend. There was a captive audience for the whole summer as there had always been, and at one time the theatres had been able to pay for the very best. And yet the books did not balance. The seaside shows were making a loss. The London-based accountants, baffled by the apparent failures forced cuts in the length of the season and advised local managers to book less costly, therefore less famous, names. The theatres, then the resorts, suffered.

Blackpool, in running its own shows, had known precisely what it was doing. More than likely, a local entrepreneur would control several businesses in the town, so could afford to lose on the early weeks of a long-running star-studded season. Hoteliers, too, felt a bond with the local businessmen and could publicise (some said make or break) a show by word of mouth among their guests.

In any case, styles were changing. At one time seeing a live show featuring a big star would be the thrill of a lifetime. A George Formby film seen five years after its making in the local flea-pit could not compare with seeing him 'live', and radio and black-and-white television could never give the gloss and glamour of a big variety spectacular. Three-channel colour television and the boom in club entertainment changed all that. The people of Batley, for instance, could see Shirley Bassey down the road at the Variety Club and television paraded the top talent every night of the week.

The holiday abroad was also becoming available; it was actually possible to holiday in Majorca as cheaply as in Morecambe—and the weather was guaranteed. MacKay had asserted in that 1935 Morecambe Guide that:

> The glory of England is in the changes in the weather and the constancy of its climate. Holiday-makers in this green and pleasant land know that (while they hope to sun bathe, and sojourn under sunny skies from morn till eve) it's all a matter of luck and the weather might be decidedly unkind.

The holidaymaker of the 1930s had no choice and was prepared to take a chance. If he lived in a mill town at least all his neighbours would have suffered from the same 'poor week'. Not so his counterpart in the 1970s. He wanted sun—and if half the street was to come back from Marbella or Torremolinos with burned backs, peeling noses and queasy stomachs he wasn't going to be left out.

Leisure was also becoming much more active and personal. Sports facilities were no longer limited to the 'red rec'—a bomb-site at the corner of the street with goal posts painted on a stripped gable end; towns were building sports centres and playing fields and exposure on television brought successive crazes for ten-pin bowling, skateboarding, tennis, ice and then roller skating. Staunchly working-class councils built municipal squash courts and Rossendale built a dry ski slope.

Increased mobility by car and motorcycle meant that the Great Outdoors was on the doorstep of every town-trapped Northerner. It had always been possible to virtually stroll out of the shadow of the mills and foundries, but now it was possible to travel further afield—to climb, sail, hang-glide, water-ski and windsurf, and these sports appealed strongly to the male image in the North. No longer content to simply spectate, the inhabitants of Rochdale and Brighouse, St Helens and Wakefield set out to discover their own countryside.

The mid-seventies marked a watershed. Fuel costs rocketed and the traditional industries of the North began to decline. The 'scale' of life contracted and the local areas benefited at the expense of the coastal towns. A newly-opened country park in the Pennines went from a few hundred visitors to the seventh most popular in the country, with upwards of 200,000 visitors a year in four years. The Piece Hall, the architectural gem of Halifax was restored and turned into a craft centre and museum complex. It found itself with 300,000 visitors a year. Hebden Bridge, the tumbling town in the Calder Valley in West Yorkshire developed a tourist trade in a handful of years.

The combination of holidays abroad and weekends near home hit the coastal resorts hard. Change was inevitable, and the resorts of the Lancashire Coast *have* adapted, some more successfully than others. The self-catering holiday is universally available (and many of the one-time 'wakey-wakey' holiday camps have adopted a more leisurely style with self-catering flats and chalets with colour television, private bathrooms and maid service). The Mayfair Hotel in Morecambe which, in 1957 proclaimed itself 'The Largest Unlicensed Hotel in Morecambe' now, with equal force, announces that it is a 'Fully Licensed Free House' with three bars and has private bathrooms, residents' lounge and sun lounge, radios and room call service, large car park—and the all-important Fire Certificate.

The bar—with its late-night bar snacks—is a necessity in the smaller establishments; economic survival depends on it, even though it can mean a 19-hour day for the proprietors. If the talent is available (and in these days of a contracting entertainment industry it often is) a small hotel will add an electronic organ or nightly singalong to its attractions. Where the establishment cannot install a lift it will often fit a 'stairslift' for the occasional disabled guest. To the usual facilities even the small hotels have added a choice of menu, shaver points and tea-makers in rooms. Some, to compensate for MacKay's 'decidedly unkind' weather have installed Sun Beds, and the sauna is by no means uncommon. Personal service is still the order of the day—an important consideration since the days when 'the Misses Fawley' placed their name above the address of their apartment house in Albert Road, Morecambe, and found it 'meaningful' to point out that they were 'Late of Oldham'. In the fifties Mr and Mrs W. Gray add their names formally at the end of their advert for the Hollymount Private Hotel; in the eighties the same address is 'Bel Air' and Garry and Rita Jarman assure that a 'warm Welcome Awaits You'.

Epilogue

Southport isn't, strictly speaking, Lancashire any more, but part of
the Borough of Sefton in the Metropolitan County of Merseyside.
The new county announces itself through the buses, and the electric
trains defiantly labelled 'Merseyrail'; it seems that *that* and little
else ties Southport to the land of Penny Lane and Cammell-Laird.
Southport was elegant and the elegance has been transposed to up-
market leisure. Bingo, rock and chips exist, but carefully fenced in
(between Lord Street and the Promenade, but visible from
neither).

Everything is newly-painted—often white—and well-kept, nurtured by a fairly affluent local authority and community. The
marine lakes are still huge, now speckled with wind-surfers as well
as dinghy-sailors and motor-boating holidaymakers. The Cambridge Hall is now the Arts Centre, the theatre on the sea-front is
new. The beach—mile after mile of it—is still the favourite place to
park; families picnic by their vehicles, giving the beach a curiously
Californian air. The fine sand that proved so troublesome in the
early days still drifts up over the outer marine road. There is a
deafening roller disco on the Pier and nearby an open-air arena
where a mezzo-soprano serenades a sun-kissed audience with 'Deep
in the Night There's a Little Brown Bird Singing'. Many towns
would have discarded such an attraction years ago. Southport
hasn't—and is the better for it. So Southport has adapted well to
the changed circumstances.

Across the Ribble estuary St Annes-on-the-Sea looks out—a
little wistfully perhaps—towards Southport. With thirty per cent
of the resident population over retirement age, the Council (now
that of the Fylde Borough) made a conscious decision to keep down
the rates and did so by cutting back on the town's potential as a

holiday resort. St Annes was also extraordinarily unlucky—fire destroyed most of its Pier and all of its theatre, the venue for an annual summer show. Apart from the new pier-head amusement arcade, St Annes remains much as it was in the 1930s. The whimsical alpine gardens on the seafront still have the twisting paths, bridges and stepping stones that are a delight for any child with an imagination, and the walk along the seafront to Fairhaven and Lytham is still a delightful experience. But delight is not enough and hoteliers complain that they have to advise their visitors to go to Blackpool for entertainment. All the same, St Annes retains a *gentleness* that is attractive.

After St Annes, Morecambe comes as a surprise. Admittedly the Winter Gardens are sadly degraded, the Midland Hotel doesn't gleam as it would if it were in Southport and the town is fighting to keep its last live theatre. (The Royalty went some time ago, which is a pity, because apart from the fact that it was designed by Frank Matcham, it once had a manager called Hird who had a clever daughter called Thora!) But Morecambe has faced up to the changed circumstances of the 1980s. The Super Swimming Stadium, 'as modern' the 1935 Guide said 'as next year's radios or cars', has gone, and in its place is the Leisure Park, which houses an open air—but heated—swimming pool complete with a wave machine, and picnic areas, bars, cafés, sunbathing terraces and the Superdome (which houses everything from roller-skating to old time dancing). It is all in a style that would not look out of place in Beverley Hills or *Star Wars 4*. It is neat, compact, excellent in every way and the kind of attraction every town, seaside or not, could benefit from.

A recent survey suggested that a family of four looking for a three-bedroom detached house would find Morecambe the cheapest place in Britain—Morecambe is still a town of value-for-money, still 'Bradford-on-Sea'. It also has the largest Ferris wheel in Europe—150ft of it, soaring over the town. It is a controversial structure, but it proves, at least, that there are still individuals prepared to lock horns with the nameless, faceless mediocrity of the town hall.

Heysham still has its predictably quaint village street, still its nettle drink (no longer called 'beer', thanks to the nameless, faceless mediocrity of the Licensing Laws). The mists of legend still swirl around the ruins of St Patrick's chapel on the headland, obscuring the silhouette of the nuclear power station just along the coast. Heysham harbour itself faced disaster when the Irish boats were withdrawn, and the Isle of Man service was no substitute. Now both it and Fleetwood are to be used in connection with the development of the Morecambe Bay gas field.

One way to get back to Morcambe from Heysham is by way of the tractor-hauled 'train' that trundles along the beach, in and out of the tidal channels, picking its way round the rocks. In the league tables of resorts Morcambe could be said to have adapted well. 'Activity' is the order of the day and Morecambe has cycling festivals, a 'Western Day', bowls tournaments, sea-angling competitions, windsurfing and power boat championships.

Fleetwood, always less reliant on the holiday trade than other towns on the coast, has suffered a number of body-blows to its traditional fishing interests—and it shows. The couples sitting in their cars on the seafront are enjoying the triple delights of retirement, summer sunshine and easy parking, but they are not contributing financially to the town. Fleetwood, remote at the end of its peninsula has an attractive feel to it—a 'separateness' and a different mixture of history, landscape and people. If there is a curiously lifeless feel about St Annes, here, at the other end of the Fylde Coast, there is a feeling of indecision. Fleetwood is now part of the vast Borough of Wyre reaching inland as far as the hills and split by the river estuary. It seems to have disorientated the town. Yet it remains, with its memories of Decimus Burton, Hesketh Fleetwood and their grand vision, one of the most under-rated towns in Lancashire.

Thornton Cleveleys, always fearful of being absorbed by Blackpool, was swallowed up by the Borough of Wyre instead. It has lost its Edwardian hydro, once the envy of the coast, its open air arena theatre and its identity as a neatly-scaled family resort. But it is still the nearest thing to a traditional family resort there is and it is still—decidedly—*not* Blackpool.

Thornton remains the kind of village usually found much further inland; both it and Cleveleys keep their separate identities and share a common, unhurried way of life. Here, as in St Annes, a substantial proportion of the resident population is over retirement age; but this is not an 'old' town—merely a settled one.

And then there's Blackpool, defying any rating in the league table of adaptability. A resort with three entertainment centres which loses one faces disaster; Blackpool could lose half a dozen and hardly notice they'd gone. Yet Blackpool has lost something—or rather it lost it for a while and is only now finding it again. The Golden Mile is gone, and what has come in its place is tatty, tasteless and simply not disreputable enough!

The Pleasure Beach whirls on—every inch packed with new rides and old and new sensations. It has 'joined the Revolution', with Britain's first 360 degree roller coaster, catapult assisted through a complete circle of steel. The Thompson family still presides—as it does now over the other funfairs at Morecambe and Southport. And as a gesture towards the deepening depression of the eighties the Pleasure Beach offered a package deal—and gave the River Caves a bright new face!

For a while, Blackpool let others dictate what was good for it, and it has always been at its best with a home-grown product; Sykes and Lumb, Lindsay Parkinson, Sergenson, Bickerstaffe and Thompson proved that (as others proved it in other towns). The Financial Director of an entertainment empire with a London address would never have allowed the Tower Ballroom; he would have insisted on something more modest, more adaptable, more easily disposable. Fortunately, they didn't think that way in Blackpool in 1894—or in any of the coastal towns from the day they were conceived right up to the present.

Late at night, as the last tram hums down Blackpool's New South Promenade to Starr Gate and the sea reaches sleepily across the beach, there is a sense of something hanging in the air. It is a sense of music waiting for the composer's pen, magic waiting for the magician's fingers. It is as intangible as the word 'pleasure', yet it was this intangible that made the resorts what they are. That is a thought well worth facing the future for!

Index

Allen, William, 10, 37
Alsop, W., 23
Apartments system, 183

Bathing regulations, 25, 40, 46
Baynard, C. E., 13
Bean, W. G., 150–2
Blackpool, 16–21, 43–5, 60–6, 79–112, 132–57, 171–6
  Airport, 76, 141
  Bourne Crescent, 144, 163, 183
  Bourne, Maud, 144, 182
  Casino building, 156–7, 164
  Claremont Park, 62, 139
  'Dreadnoughts', 82, 96–7
  Emberton, Joseph, 152–6
  Golden Mile, 84, 99–136, 146
  Grand Theatre, 108, 110, 119, 180
  Gypsies, 133–5
  Holland, Bill, 30, 105, 118
  Holroyd Smith, M., 80
  Hotels, 17, 18–21, 45, 62, 102, 163–70, 192
  Hutton (family), 18–21
  Illuminations, 114, 144, 171–6
  Improvement Act (1917), 89, 137
  John Bull, 130–1
  Luff, Walter, 93–7
  Lumb, T., 88, 92–3, 95, 120, 198
  Matcham, Frank, 102, 106–11, 196
  Opera House, 106, 119, 148
  Outhwaite, J. W., 150–1
  Piers, 62, 81, 116, 119, 132, 139, 148
  Pleasure Beach, 89, 90, 132, 149–57, 164, 171, 174, 175, 198
  Quin, R. C., 82

Raikes Hall (and gardens), 45, 116–18
Railways, 47, 60–1, 62, 65, 87, 88, 134
Randle, Frank, 114–16
Singleton Thorpe, 63
Squires Gate, 141, 142, 165; *see also* Airport
Stanley Park, 90, 140, 144, 147
Sykes, B., 88, 92, 93, 120, 198
Theatres, 99–136, 143, 146, 148, 180
Tower, 72, 100, 106, 110, 112–14, 117, 119, 140
Trams, 79–98, 119–31, 132, 139, 151, 166, 173, 174, 198
Blackpool & Fleetwood Tramroad, 83, 89, 94, 119–31, 151, 166
Blackpool–Lytham railway, 62, 65
Bourne, Maud, 144, 177, 182
Burton, Decimus, 52 71, 126, 197
Byrom, John, 11, 12

Canals, 22, 32, 40
Casino building (Blackpool), 156–7, 164
Civil War (Fylde Campaign, 10, 35, 69
Claremont Park, 63, 139
Cleveleys, 93, 119, 121, 125, 126–7, 130, 191, 197–8
Cleveleys Park, 93, 126–7
Dutch Cottage, 127
Trams, 119, 121, 125, 126–7, 130
Clifton (family), 35, 38, 72
Clifton Estate, 71

Dalton (family), 10–11
Derby, Earls of, 35–8, 140
Docks, and harbours, 42, 52,

55–7, 178, 179, 182, 197
'Dreadnoughts', 82, 96–7

Emberton, Joseph, 152–6
English Electric Company, 93–5

Fleetwood, 51–9, 60, 69, 84, 87, 89, 119–31, 197
Blackpool & Fleetwood Tramroad, 58, 83, 89, 94, 119–31, 151, 166
Burton, Decimus, 52–71, 126, 197
Docks, 52, 55–7, 197
Garstang & Knott End Railway, 87, 128
Hesketh-Fleetwood, Peter, 52, 60, 69
Preston & Wyre Railway, 48, 55–6, 60
Railways, 87, 88, 128
Rossall, 10, 37, 52, 93, 125
Santa Ana, 35–8
Wyre, Borough of, 33, 127, 197
Wyre, River, 14, 35, 42, 51, 57
Floyer, John, 13
Fylde, Borough of, 33, 195
Fylde, The, 14, 16, 34, 40, 42, 61, 113, 114

Garstang & Knott End Railway, 87, 128
Glasson Dock, 42, 179
Golden Mile, 84, 99–136, 146
'Graf Zeppelin', 147
Grand Theatre, Blackpool, 108, 110, 119, 180
Gypsies, 133–5

Hawthorne, Nathaniel, 27
Headlands Hotel, Blackpool, 163–70
Hesketh-Fleetwood, Peter, 52, 60, 69

Heysham *see* Morecambe and Heysham
Heysham Harbour, 179, 182, 197
Holland, Bill, 30, 105, 118
Holroyd Smith, M., 80
Hutton (family), 18–21

Illuminations, Blackpool, 114, 144, 171–6

Jacobites, 11–13
Johnson, Amy, 141

Lancashire & Yorkshire Railway, 27, 33, 55–6, 60, 87–8, 128, 134, 189
Lancaster, 11, 15, 34, 172, 182
Lancaster Canal, 42, 179
Leeds & Liverpool Canal, 22, 32, 40
'Little North Western' Railway, 178
Liverpool, 27, 31, 33
Luff, Walter, 93–8
Lumb, T., 88 92–3, 95, 120, 198
Lytham St Annes, 16, 33, 34, 39–48, 64–5, 69–78, 81, 84, 89, 91, 119, 139, 195, 197
Bathing, 40, 46
Blackpool Airport, 76, 141
Blackpool–Lytham Railway, 62, 65
Clifton (family), 35, 38, 72
Clifton Estate, 71
Land and Building Company, 71–2
Piers, 75
Porritt, W. J., 73–8
Trams, 81, 90, 91, 132

Mancunian Films, 115
Matcham, Frank, 102, 106–11, 180, 196
Merseyside Metropolitan

County, 33, 195
Midland Railway, 128, 179, 181
Morecambe and Heysham, 31, 33, 113, 156, 173, 177–88, 192, 194, 196
Bourne, Maude, 177, 182
Harbour, 178
Heysham Harbour, 179, 182, 197
Illuminations, 173
Leisure Park, 196
Matcham, Frank, 180, 196
Piers, 180, 191
Pleasure Park, 198
Railways, 128, 178–9, 181
Royalty Theatre, 180, 196
Tower, 113, 180
Trams, 181
Morecambe Bay, 15, 35

North West Central Railway, 33

Opera House (Blackpool), 106, 119, 148
Outhwaite, J. W., 150–1

Piers, 28, 62, 74, 77, 114, 116, 119, 132, 139, 148, 180, 191, 196
Pleasure Beach (Blackpool), 89, 90, 132, 149–57, 164, 171, 174, 175, 198
Pleasure Park (Morecambe), 198
Porritt, W. J., 73–8
Preston, 11, 15, 36, 42, 44
Preston & Wyre Railway, 47–8, 55–6, 60

Quin, R. C., 82

Raikes Hall (and Gardens), 45, 116–18
Railways, 27, 28, 31–2, 33, 47, 48, 55, 60, 62, 65, 87, 88, 128, 134, 178–9, 181, 189, 195

Randle, Frank, 114–16
Ribble, River, 14, 22, 35, 42, 64, 84, 195
Rickards, C. F., 163–70
Rossall, 10, 37, 52, 93, 125
Royalty Theatre (Morecambe), 180, 196

St Annes-on-Sea *see* Lytham St Annes
Santa Ana, 35–8
Sefton, Borough of, 33, 195
Sergenson, Thomas, 105–6
Singleton Thorpe, 63
Southport, 7, 22–38, 47, 65, 177, 195, 198
Bathing Regulations, 25
Canals, 22, 32
Hawthorne, Nathaniel, 27
Railways, 27, 28, 31, 32, 33, 128
Pier, 28
Sutton, William, 22–3
Spencer, Earl, 175
Squires Gate, 141, 165
Stanley Park, 90, 140, 144, 147
Stoll, Oswald, 107
Sutton, William, 22–3
Sykes, Benjamin, 88, 92, 93, 120, 198

Theatres, 100–10, 180, 195, 196
Thompson, Leonard, 88, 152–3, 158, 174, 198
Towers, 72, 100, 106, 110, 112–14, 117, 119, 140, 180
Trams, 79–98, 119–31, 132, 151, 166, 173, 174, 181, 198
Tyldesley (family), 10

Wyre, Borough of, 33, 127, 197
Wyre, River, 14, 35, 42, 51, 57